Sarada Ramakrishna Vivekananda
Associations of Oregon,
San Francisco,
& Hawaii

DISSOLVING THE MINDSTREAM

WITHDRAWING THE WORLDS OF NAME AND FORM IN TIME AND SPACE, IN MEDITATION

Babaji Bob Kindler

©2014   Babaji Bob Kindler
All rights reserved.
Published by SRV Associations

No part of this book may be reproduced in any manner without written permission of the author or publisher except for quotations embodied in articles or reviews. For further information write to:

SRV Associations
P.O. Box 1364
Honoka'a, Hawaii 96727
srvinfo@srv.org   www.srv.org
            or
SRV Hawaii
P.O. Box 380
Paauilo, HI., 96776 USA

The publication of this book was made possible by donations from friends and students of the SRV Associations.

Printed in the United States of America

ISBN 978-1-891893-14-8

Acknowledgements:
Our thanks to Rama Nand Tiwari for usage of the cover image.

Contents

Introduction xi

Chapter One — Emptiness: Empty of What? 1

Chapter Two — Curtain of Nescience, Cloud of Unknowing 16

Chapter Three — The Secret of Comprehensive Meditation ... 34

Chapter Four — Emanation & Dissolution in Vedic Cosmology ... 48

Chapter Five — Seven Levels of Cause and Effect 61

Chapter Six — A Simple Overview 70

Chapter Seven — The Unreal Never Is, The Real Never Ceases To Be 78

Chapter Eight — Total Dissolution of the Mindstream 84

Sanskrit Glossary 99

List of Illustrations/Charts

The Dissolution of the Mindstream 3

Phases and Permutations of the All-Pervasive Prana 7

The Meaning of Objects. 11

Curtain of Nescience, Cloud of Unknowing. 19

The Three Levels of Sankalpa and Vikalpa 31

Two Forms and Eight Types of Meditation 37

Omkara — The Great Cause 49

Vedic Triputis and Quintuplications. 51

The Five Akashas of Vedic Philosophy 55

Dasabhumikas — The Ten Pure Lands 59

Causality, Origins, and Reincarnation 63

Phases of the Soul in Relativity 69

The Seer, the Seen, the Unseen, and the Obscene 71

The Integral Constitution of the Luminaries 73

The Disappearance of Ignorance 81

The Dissolution of the Mindstream (repeat) 85

Chidabhasa — The Reflection of Brahman in the Cosmos 87

Dedication

To all intrepid spiritual travelers who sincerely practice the art of meditation.

Sivaratri, 2013

Introduction

The mind plunges into formlessness on four occasions: first, in deep sleep; second, in the event of physical death; third (if one holds a meditation practice) when the mind experiences the sudden or gradual absence of thought; and lastly, in that rare and inexplicable instance called *samadhi* by the seers of Truth. All four of these states of formlessness should be contemplated, and it is best if such ruminations are subjected to the counsel of the wise *(guru-anushasana)*, the words of the illumined souls called revealed scripture *(vidyashastra)*, and a healthy and ever ongoing effort at personal spiritual experience *(aparokshanubhuti)* brought about by *sadhana* — purificatory self-effort.

It is evident by the above words that one is not to wait for death in order to enter into inspection of one's own consciousness. As the scriptures tell us, scrutinizing human awareness and thereby searching for signs of inner Essence is rather like culling wheat from chaff, churning milk to get butter, subjecting wood to friction in order to get fire, or pressing hundreds of sesame seeds to get a few drops of oil. Analogies such as these from the scriptures reveal that mankind's Essence is extremely subtle, and that it will take an equally subtle method to draw It out from the many layers of covering (desire, passion, karma, nescience, etc.) that conceal It.

But the main aim of this book intends to take the striving human soul far beyond a mere revelation that such Essence exists. In India, and unlike western countries and their philosophies, it was never a question of whether "God" existed or not, but rather an adamant declaration that "God Is Existence." This also infers that all existence Is God — *Sarvam Khalvidam Brahman*. Based on such firm footing, and upon eternal axioms that are both universally accepted and incontrovertible, the seers of Mother India moved to demonstrate this truth in life.

And this "life" is mind. Everything proceeds from mind. As the Holy Mother, Sri Sarada Devi, has stated: *"Objects are just thought made concretized."* When the human mind vibrates with thought, all worlds spring forth. It is all a matter of what level of mind one is speaking about — cosmic, collective, or individual. The first operates at a causal level; the second, at a subtle level; and the last, at a gross level. People, individuals, can hardly imagine that their world is the result of a massive confluence of multi-leveled vibrations that are the mental processes of ancestors, celestials, gods and goddesses, sages, saints, and seers, and The Trinity. It is a mass of vibration — good, bad, and mixed.

It was the realization around this pregnant *"triputi"* that caused beings like Sri Krishna, Lord Buddha, and Jesus Christ, to seek a way out of the vibratory realms, and beyond the crushing weight of rebirth in heaven and earth that mankind and his ancestors suffer in rounds. Whether they had to resort to a cave for a time, sit under a tree for weeks, or take up habitation in the wilderness for awhile, such vision came to them as to compel them to go beyond form. And whether they called it *Samadhi, Nirvana,* or *Beatific Vision,* the special facet of It was the disappearance of mind, its thought, and therefore its "vibrations" — *vrittis, spandas, The Word, Sphota,* or *AUM*. In other words, *"In the beginning"* the Word broke into vibration and the worlds emerged from It (gross state). When *"....The Word was with God,"* the process of involution or dissolution was under way (subtle/causal states). And when *"....The Word was God,"* there were no realms of name and form, or they were all held in abeyance and there was only *That* — Pure Consciousness; Timeless, Deathless Awareness; Nondual Samadhi.

As was already mentioned, the seeker after Truth must not wait for the formlessness of death to overtake the embodied condition, but must look ahead, and behind, for clues and precognition of what the seers call "apparent" emptiness. Beyond merely calling up post-natal experiences in the crib, the meditator must search the mind for pre-natal memories, as well as for record of past lifetimes. This will constitute a start towards viewing what the seers describe as *smriti-bedhu* — a causal memory stored deep in the inner reaches of the mind. It is rather like a "trail of breadcrumbs" that one left for oneself early on, so that a process of connecting the dots, cosmically speaking, could be undertaken later. This would ensure that the transmigrating soul could save itself from pointless wandering in the worlds of name and form under the cruel influence of *maya/samsara*, and always experience the rejuvenating state of conscious formlessness so healthy for the soul and its natural resilience — a form of crucial health that, for those not in possession of a meditative practice, can only be had in this world in the form of deep sleep.

Other than deep sleep and death, then — both occurring in most individuals randomly and unconsciously — the superlative stations of meditation *(dhyana)* and nonduality *(samadhi)* have remained open and largely untapped throughout time. In both the teachings and the teachers of these most subtle attainments, there lie instructions specific to the title of this book — *Dissolving the Mindstream*. The chart visual on page 3 states, that in both the Vedanta and the Yoga *darshanas* there is a classic method with which to effect this essentially spiritual end. It is based in even more ancient darshanas (ways of clear seeing) like *Sankhya Yoga* and its famous enumeration of cosmic principles. The forthcoming chapters and their respective charts revolve around and explain to the sedulous seeker how to undertake and operate what has been called by the luminaries of various traditions as the *"destruction of the mind's waves,"* the *"involution of all objective phenomena,"* and the *"withdrawal of all mental projection" (sankalpa)* back into the primal source from whence it came. It is to this end that we must turn our intense scrutiny.

Chapter One

Emptiness — Empty Of What?

The inscrutable term, "emptiness," or *shunyata*, utilized in Buddhist and Vedantic philosophies, is often perplexing and disconcerting to the novitiate and beginning aspirant. Advanced practitioners often fail to comprehend it, and worldly-minded beings will not even attempt to understand such an abstruse principle of refined philosophy. Even intelligent human beings, like many quantum physicists, for instance, fail to comprehend it. More shall be said on this later.

Similarly, unusual terms such as *"neti neti"* in Vedanta, and *"atma vichara"* in Advaita, call up a "blank" in the mind in this regard, and therefore need to be examined. Pertaining to the latter, atma vichara, or inquiry into the nature of the self/Self, the question "Who am I?" is brought to the fore for contemplation. The tendency today, in both teachers and practitioners of atma vichara, is to ask this question over and over, ad nauseum, yet never come up with any answer, and never embark upon a method that has one arriving at a definitive end or foundational and reliable conclusion.

Who am I?, Neti Neti, and Iti Iti

Among teachers in the know — gurus, acharyas, preceptors — an answer to the above question is ever forthcoming, and an apt conclusion has been reached. The inquirer must come to know <u>what I am not</u> before he can understand <u>who I am</u>. In other words, one is not the body, the five gross elements, the five subtle elements, the ten senses, the *prana* (life-force), or the fourfold mind (dual mind, thought, intelligence, and ego). Briefly put, I am not the many Cosmic Principles/Tattvas that Sankhya Yoga reveals for scrutiny and meditation in order that we withdraw the universe of name and form in space and time back within us. As Shankaracharya has exclaimed so succinctly in his scripture, the *Vivekachudamani*: *"Brahman is an indeterminable mass of pure, conscious Awareness, ever-perfect and ever-free. Therefore, taking what is external and what is internal, render them both into one indivisible state. Then meditate upon that blissfully singular state, pass your time contentedly, and be free."*

In Vedanta, neti neti (not this, not this) begins here, and proceeds inward to join with and penetrate the realm of the Trinity *(Lords Brahma, Vishnu, and Siva)*, "Unmanifested Prakriti" (nature/subtle matter held in abeyance in a causal condition), and then The Word, in precise fashion and with methodical precision. This should not be taken only as a mere statement on the evolution and involution of the entire cosmic process from The Word on out, but more as a specific command to the spiritual seeker from the enlightened ones to engage and master this process consciously in meditation, all within the very mind that formulated it in the first place. Only then will the soul know its intrinsic part in the projection of the universes, inner and outer, and will thereby destroy false assumptions that have accumulated over lifetimes, assumptions such as "God created the universe," "The world is all that exists," "Matter is the only Reality," "Nothing exists after death," and other fallacious beliefs. In this way, both theology and science have a lot to learn.

Further, this dissolution process all consummates in full realization, or Samadhi, as described by that seldom heard Vedantic phrase, *"iti iti,"* which translates as "all this, all this." What the sincere seeker finds, then, is Divine Reality — Brahman. Thus, a positive end to the "not this, not this" process arrives, and an answer to the question "Who am I" is found.

The Nonself — What We Are Not

The chart on the facing page (page 3), which will be our main go-to image for this book, reveals this entire involution

Dissolving the Mind Stream
The Formless Meditation of the Upanisads

"When a sugar cube dissolves into hot liquid, it first breaks in half, then into small chunks, then into granules, and finally there is nothing left but sweet liquid. Similarly, when the mind moves towards authentic meditation, it first contemplates the dual world, then the many teachings, then living particles of its own intelligence, and finally enters full immersion. What remains then is one blissful, indivisible homogenous mass of pure, conscious Awareness." — Babaji Bob Kindler

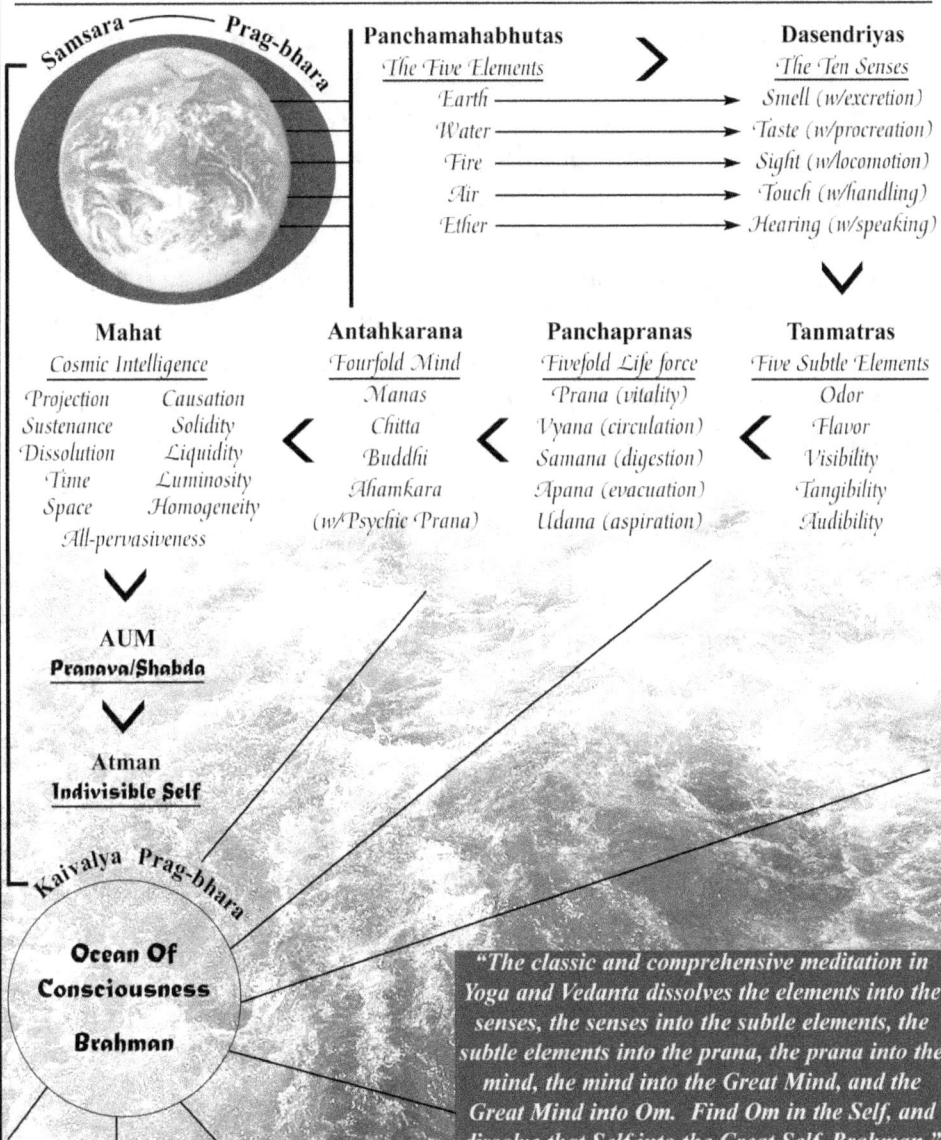

Samsara — Prag-bhara

Panchamahabhutas
The Five Elements
- Earth → Smell (w/excretion)
- Water → Taste (w/procreation)
- Fire → Sight (w/locomotion)
- Air → Touch (w/handling)
- Ether → Hearing (w/speaking)

Dasendriyas
The Ten Senses

Mahat
Cosmic Intelligence
- Projection
- Sustenance
- Dissolution
- Time
- Space
- Causation
- Solidity
- Liquidity
- Luminosity
- Homogeneity
- All-pervasiveness

Antahkarana
Fourfold Mind
- Manas
- Chitta
- Buddhi
- Ahamkara
- (w/ Psychic Prana)

Panchapranas
Fivefold Life force
- Prana (vitality)
- Vyana (circulation)
- Samana (digestion)
- Apana (evacuation)
- Udana (aspiration)

Tanmatras
Five Subtle Elements
- Odor
- Flavor
- Visibility
- Tangibility
- Audibility

AUM
Pranava/Shabda

Atman
Indivisible Self

Kaivalya — Prag-bhara

Ocean Of Consciousness — Brahman

"The classic and comprehensive meditation in Yoga and Vedanta dissolves the elements into the senses, the senses into the subtle elements, the subtle elements into the prana, the prana into the mind, the mind into the Great Mind, and the Great Mind into Om. Find Om in the Self, and dissolve that Self into the Great Self, Brahman."

Chart by Babaji Bob Kindler — Property of SRV Associations

process clearly for the practitioner. Beginning with the earth, where embodied beings are both in abundance and in bondage, the observant seeker must note the five elements. These are known to all, but in a superficial way, and are always taken for granted. Few actually meditate upon these five from the inward standpoint and trajectory, and if they are studied at all, they are seen in the end as building blocks of the external universe, never as manifestations (effects) of subtler principles (causes).

It may be mentioned here, that when science looks into a fragment of matter to behold a mass of vibrating particles, which are changing at the rate of a billionth of a second, they are not looking inward at all, but further outward. There is no further out to go, in fact, which demonstrates both Vedanta's "unreality of the world" contention *(Brahman satya, jagad mithya)*, and Buddhism's *shunyata*, or "emptiness" assertion. To refer to Christ's own way of stating this, we must not build our houses on the shifting sands, i.e., particles, of this world, but on the bedrock of the Spirit. This is why *"Birds have nests and foxes have holes, but the son of Man hath no place here to lay his head."* The seers thus suggest gaining an inner life. That will require a mental movement from the gross world to the subtle worlds within.

The Real Building Blocks: A Series of Quintuplications

Referring back to the chart on the previous page, we find the five elements in direct correlation with the five senses of knowledge and the five active senses. Meditating on these to make helpful connections — like smell with earth, water with taste, fire with sight, etc. — we learn just how far afield man has ventured by not making these connections with nature, resulting in a scattered and imbalanced mind that covets possessions, seeks pleasure, attaches to objects, and even goes so far as to war against others in order to dominate over them to secure "empty" materials. In addition to all this, we also find that we cannot rely upon the senses to give us a rendering of what is beyond their power to reveal. Either way they look — outward into space, further outward into vibrating material particles, inward into daydreams, fantasies, emotions, and passions, or further inward towards the *"kingdoms of heaven within,"* the five senses fail to illumine or enlighten us. A sensualist, a hedonist, a materialist, and the intellectual thus all fall short of realizing their divine nature, which is beyond origins and mental overlays.

It is only when these fifteen insentient principles, which are outer building blocks of a still undetected inner process, are well connected in meditation, and then placed further within – the true inside – on the origins (not the evolutes) of gross matter, that some early clues are gained. Here is the first missing link in modern man's limited scientific understanding, called the *tanmatras* in the ancient Sanskrit. Though insentient themselves, they are nevertheless imbued with something of a subtler nature, revealing an internal bridge between the gross elements and these origins that will assist the soul later in connecting the five senses with their inner powers (power of the eyes to see, power of the ears to hear, etc.). Cause and effect in the physical sense only, then, is such a tiny part of the cosmic picture. Cause and effect in the mind (not the brain) begins to unfold subtler truths.

These twenty principles listed so far, part of an amazing and ever-burgeoning quintuplication process, form most of the superlative host of Sankhya's cosmic principles which, when connected to the mind (which is fourfold by the way – mind, thought, intelligence, and ego), complete the collection. The mind, too, could be included in the quintuplication enumeration if the cosmic mind, *Mahat*, were counted; but its origin is much earlier. The real question to be asked at this point is what is left unaccounted for that connects the five tanmatras to the mind at this subtlemost level? Here is where prana, life force itself, must be taken into account in the practitioner's meditation process.

Prana: A Serious Missing Link in Western Thinking

Along with the tanmatras, but more crucial of understanding, is *prana*. In the yogic tradition, and to date in the West, *"the single prana in its five forms"* has been taught at the physical level only, which is due to a gross oversight by those poor representatives of spirituality who are caught up in concerns for the body, its health, its food, and its exercises only — what to speak of the money to be made from these — and who thereby leave the term and principle of "wholism" lacking of its most important ingredients. Besides the *psychic prana*, which is often seized upon prematurely by all who give up the spiritual quest early to court lower phenomena (hatha yogis, occultists, etc.), there is also the energy called *mukhya prana*, a *sattvic* energy that is taken up and sublimated by inward ascending yogis *(urdhvaretoyogi)* who strive to utilize that refined substance called *Ojas*, subtle spiritual energy. Ojas, in turn, duly reveals *Tejas*, of infinite shining power, a special Intelligence *(Buddhi)* that science and materialism will never be able to account for. Endless spiritual wisdom and teachings flow from it, along with revelation of origins far beyond such limited ideologies as the "Big Bang" theory, the Seven-day Creation Theory, the untenable idea of a creation out of nothing, and others. This Intelligence is the first principle out of the gate at the time of initial mental projection, and the "first compound," containing a combination of Brahman, The Word, and God's Mind — Mahat.

    On the facing page, and not forgetting the chart on page 3, the reader can see another chart on the inscrutable principle of Prana. Since prana has been used in the scriptures to describe everything from energy in food all the way up to the formless Brahman, it is then no wonder that there is confusion around it and its workings — these conundrums rising only if one happens to come across and study the principle in the first place. Suffice to say that it is this prana in its subtler forms that, among other functions, carry transmigrating souls in and out of embodiment (via subtle nerves) and to regions beyond the physical universe.

    Looking briefly at food first, we must respect that Christ made that cryptic statement, *"Man does not live by bread alone."* Some aver that he was speaking of the Spirit at that moment, that man lives really by the Spirit. But this opinion does not hold water, philosophically speaking. God, Brahman, the Formless Reality, is never found in form; It is completely beyond any type

Phases & Permutations of the All-Pervasive Prana

"Controlling the heaven-aspiring senses and the life-force with the help of the mind and intellect, the Immanent Soul so regenerates them as to enable them to manifest the infinite, self-luminous Light of Awareness. All that exists in the three worlds is under the control of Prana, and Prana is Mother. May She transmit Wisdom to us via Her Divine Energy."
≈ Svetasvataropanisad

Kundalini Shakti

"Of the Atman is born the Prana. Like the shadow of a man it is spread out on That. It comes into the body by the will of the mind. The one who knows the imperishable Atman, in which rests the mind, prana, and senses, verily becomes omniscient and enters into all."

Level	Phase	Aspect
	Transcendent	
Super-Conscious		Shakti/ AUM
	Pure	
Universal		Cosmic/ Intellect
	Subtle	
Divine		Mind/ Psyche
Celestial	Refined	Sacrifice/ Gods
Ethereal		Rebirth/ Ancestors
Vital		Body & Senses
Primal	Raw	The Five Elements
Gross		Food

"When the three matras of AUM are left unconnected there is mortality, but when they are connected in the Prana they are rightfully employed. What is peaceful, undecaying, immortal, free from fear, the seer attains by the means of AUM."

"The wise one attains immortality having known the origin of the Prana, its advent, its all-pervasiveness, its fivefold distribution, and its internal aspects."

"In the heart there are a hundred-and-one nerves, and in each of them are another hundred, and these branch into seventy-two thousand more. In all of these moves the all-pervasive Prana."

"Oh Prana, Thou art the best carrier for the gods, and the first offering to the ancestors. Thou art Indra and Rudra, and the Lord of Lights."

"Through one of the great nadis the Prana carries the soul to virtuous worlds by virtuous deeds, and to sinful worlds by sinful acts — and by both to the world of men."

"To Thee, oh Prana, who dwellest in the body with the senses, all creatures carry their offerings."

"He burns as fire; He is the sun, He is the cloud and the wind, earth and all matter. He is what is and what is not, and also what is immortal."

"When Prana pours down as rain, all creatures are delighted, knowing there will be food."

"Like the rays of a setting sun, when a man sleeps, all the senses and their functions merge into the superior god called the mind. Then he hears not, sees not, smells not, tastes not, feels not, and they say 'he sleeps.' At that time the fires of Prana alone remain awake in this city, holding the two oblations of inspiration and expiration within it."
≈ Prashnopanisad

Chart by Babaji Bob Kindler   Property of SRV Associations

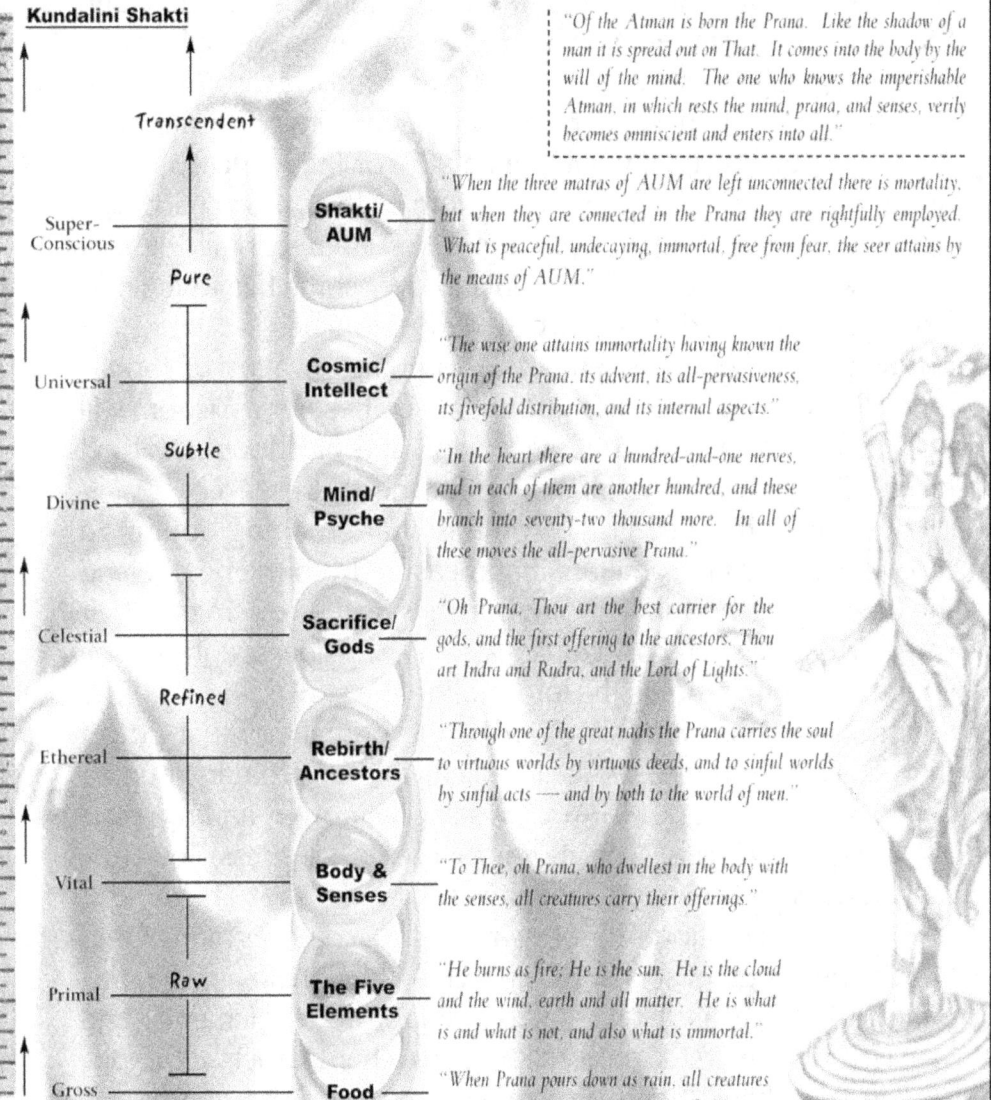

of energy or movement. It seems more likely that Jesus was speaking of subtle life-force, then. In other words, God may be the underlying foundation for Eternal Life, but in embodied life there is an energy, neither electric nor kinetic, that moves all that is unseen. It animates everything from blood flowing through the veins, to lungs breathing in and out, and even to souls transmigrating from earth to *"the kingdoms of heaven within."* An explanation of the new chart (on page 7) will demonstrate this.

To begin with, it would be helpful for the reader to reflect upon the quotes at the top and bottom of the prana chart. The *Upanisads*, the essential scriptures of Vedanta, contain all that special knowledge gained by mankind over some five to ten millennia or more, and that has been left untouched by the recent onslaught of modern science and ongoing ravages of fundamentalist religion. A copious abundance of esoteric wisdom will be revealed in this process, and many age-old doubts will get dispelled — a winning combination for the Truth seeker.

There are three graphs on this chart, running bottom to top, which act as barometers that measure both the degree and the function of the subtle pranic particles as they operate at their respective levels of consciousness. The inside graph, in the image of a spring, holds the information the soul is seeking. The spring represents *Kundalini Shakti*, the primal spiritual power that is as yet unreleased (still coiled) in the ordinary human being. Prana is a lower form of this special power, and a vehicle for Her (Kundalini is seen as the Supreme Goddess) inwardly ascending march towards Enlightenment.

Many additional quotes from the scriptures are placed beside the rungs of this spring which will help explain the gradation of prana as it takes place. Food, body, elements, and senses form the first aspects, all held together by their commonality in the physical cause of things. But one can see by the slokas placed in accord with each entry that the primal cause is not only not forgotten, nor taken for granted, but acknowledged as the underlying force behind food, body, and senses, and even propitiated and prayed to as the living god of subtler regions.

These regions, in consciousness, are first saluted as properties of the mind containing the heavens of the ancestors and the realms of the gods. Termed lower and higher heavens in Vedic Cosmology, the worlds falling within their reach and under the just jurisdiction of their respective overseers are legion. The Sanskrit words *lokas* and *akashas* form a more fitting descriptive of the abundance lying here. As the Upanisads relate, *"In all of these the prana flows."* And as the accompanying graphs infer, prana is beginning to refine to the level of *Shakti* power, transcending physical, vital, and celestial levels to reach inwardly towards an even more divine status.

It is at this divine level of awakened mind that prana reveals a new kind of life and living, one that proceeds from and flows through a subtle network of nerves (nadis) that is never suspected by the countless beings who do not discover and master the inward moving prana. And it is also here that the validation and efficacy for the *Dissolution of the Mindstream* meditation presents itself, as shown on the main chart on page 3.

To reiterate, this powerful pranic energy that is found as the basis of food, and which then gets converted into energy to sustain healthy bodies, does not end its beneficial rise there. When followed inwardly in meditation it is also found to be the invisible force via which thoughts are energized and turned further inwards towards subtle regions, and eventually to formlessness itself. This is the atmosphere of powerful ideas and inner visions, as instanced by the prana's rise into the realm of the intelligence, both collective and cosmic.

Prana, as *Shakti*, soon enters its most subtle state and dissolves into *AUM* – the Word, the "Unstruck Sound." For the one who is consciously riding the prana/shakti vehicle like a great Garuda bird, all the worlds of name and form are seen to find their dissolution in The Word. As Sri Ramakrishna has stated, *"When I first beheld the Word within me, I saw all the worlds coming forth from It and dissolving back into it simultaneously."* This is formlessness, a state of "unmanifested matter," where all particles – atomic, pranic, mental, psychic, and intellectual –

cease to vibrate. It is here where the "neti neti" process finds its culmination, and where that inscrutable word, shunyata, emptiness, reveals its higher secret.

By the term, "emptiness," the seers do not intend to infer an absolute void. Obviously, the void cannot be an absolute because we have seen it; someone has witnessed it and given it the name, "Void." Thus, it exists, as do all things. It is not nonexistent. The term "emptiness," then, refers to, 1) the lack of any abiding substance in the worlds of name and form and, 2) the inability of material things to fulfill the human mind. It does not mean that there is no witness to empty things and phenomena. Otherwise, for instance, we could not say, "I am dissatisfied." The Observer is ever present. However, if the Observer ceases the art of careful observation, it will forget itself in the press of matter and the rush of time, and the weights of cause and effect will waylay it — even lose it completely amidst what gets observed.

And that is why the practitioner engages in the process of the *Dissolution of the Mindstream* daily, until the building blocks of the Universe (not just the physical ones) are fully known, and the steps which accomplish that inward ascension of Awareness are memorized and mastered. To repeat, "In order to know who you are, you must know what you are not." Everything that changes is the nonself. That which changes not is the Self. When the witness sees and knows the process of cosmic evolution and involution, it will behold the changing and will then take steps — as all the illumined souls have done — to separate the Self from the nonself and live in eternal Perfection — *Samadhi, Nirvana, Satori*.

The Meaning of Emptiness

To aid in the teaching of shunyata, emptiness, another chart is placed for study on the facing page. In keeping with contemporary Vedantic and Buddhistic teachings (one explaining in terms of the unreality of the world, and the other describing by way of the substanceless nature of relativity) we see that there are three levels to existence — as seen in the chart. More

The Real Meaning of Objects

"Most beings, beholding physical objects such as trees, animals, planets, etc., assume them to be real, or actual. However, modern science has uncovered the atomic particle tree. Philosophy teaches about the illusory tree, its display being only an appearance. The luminaries, going deeper, speak of the Atman tree, or Buddha nature tree. Thus, there are three levels to existence: the external, the internal, and the absolute. Knowing about this triple subdivision, along with the nature of each, the human mind espies the truth about all manifestation and swiftly frees itself from bondage to objects."   Babaji Bob Kindler

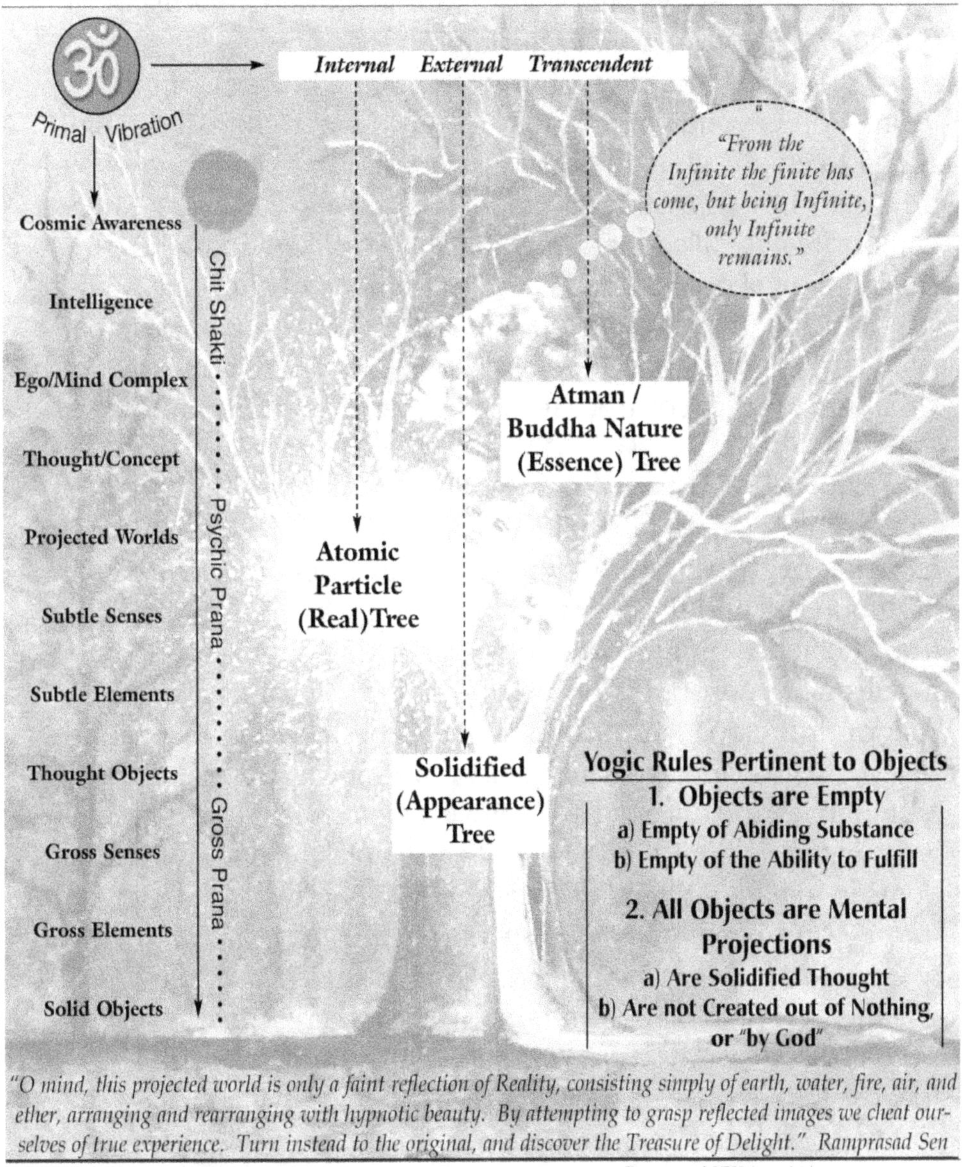

Internal   External   Transcendent

Ом — Primal Vibration

- Cosmic Awareness
- Intelligence
- Ego/Mind Complex
- Thought/Concept
- Projected Worlds
- Subtle Senses
- Subtle Elements
- Thought Objects
- Gross Senses
- Gross Elements
- Solid Objects

Chit Shakti • Psychic Prana • Gross Prana

Atomic Particle (Real) Tree

Atman / Buddha Nature (Essence) Tree

Solidified (Appearance) Tree

"From the Infinite the finite has come, but being Infinite, only Infinite remains."

Yogic Rules Pertinent to Objects

1. Objects are Empty
 a) Empty of Abiding Substance
 b) Empty of the Ability to Fulfill

2. All Objects are Mental Projections
 a) Are Solidified Thought
 b) Are not Created out of Nothing, or "by God"

"O mind, this projected world is only a faint reflection of Reality, consisting simply of earth, water, fire, air, and ether, arranging and rearranging with hypnotic beauty. By attempting to grasp reflected images we cheat ourselves of true experience. Turn instead to the original, and discover the Treasure of Delight."   Ramprasad Sen

Chart by Babaji Bob Kindler   Property of SRV Associates simply put, both Vedanta and Buddhism agree that there are two divisions, though they often vary on the terminology and a few other minor points. Whatever the case may be, the empirical side of relative existence *(vyavaharika)* covers all that is in the world and is in the mind, while only that which is transcendent *(Paramarthika)* can be called Reality, by whatever name is carefully selected – Brahman or Buddha Nature, *Purusha* or *Prajnaparam, Turiya* or *Tathagatagarbha*.

The real essence of this teaching, however, finds its expression beyond words and verbiage. On the chart, the image of the tree is used as the object in question. Its first level is its physical form consisting of wood, sap, leaves, etc. As a whole composite it is called the "appearance" tree based upon the conclusion that all objects are "unreal," or "empty" of substance. The real or actual tree, however, is a mass of vibrating particles; that is its actual existence on earth, and the latest advances of Quantum Physics corroborate this, or should corroborate it.

Purnyata – Fullness

But what about what is "Real," and what is "Full" – called *purnyata* by the ancients? That is called the "Buddha Nature" tree in Buddhism, and the "Atman" tree in Vedanta. Atman, the only true Substance – pure, conscious Awareness – infuses and permeates all things, but is not Itself a "thing." In other words, we cannot find God here on earth simply because God is not an object. Nor is God, whatever one names or calls It, an energy or a thought form/concept. Swami Vivekananda clears this up nicely in writings about the West and its peoples to one of his students in a letter written in the late 1800's, after his visit here:

"Nowhere have I heard so much about 'love, life, and liberty' as in this country, but nowhere is it less understood. Here God is either a terror or a healing power, vibration, and so forth." Continuing on in this vein in another letter, and speaking about the western mind's tendency towards objectifying Reality, he states: *"....and that this Lord we are trying to realize from time without beginning in the objective, and in the attempt throwing*

up such 'queer creatures of our fancy' as man, woman, child, body, mind, earth, sun, moon, stars, the world, love, hate, property, wealth, etc.; also ghosts, devils, angels and gods, God, etc."

This quote matches nicely with the graph on the chart under study on page 11. On the left hand side of the chart is displayed a list of cosmic principles, from gross to subtle, in inwardly ascending fashion. These "tattvas" run their course from the "solid" objects and gross elements, on through thought/dream objects, to the mind/ego complex, and on to levels of causal vibration ending up in The Word. It is from these materials that *"....creatures of our fancy such as man, woman, child, body, mind, earth, sun, moon, stars, the world, love, hate, property, wealth, ghosts, devils, angels gods, and God,"* all make their appearance. They are unreal, or empty, due to having no abiding substance. An object, states Vedanta, cannot be known, and that is simply because it consists of the grossest level of vibration, i.e., particles changing at a billionth of a second.

But the western mind has not drawn the conclusion that, because objects are all empty of substance, i.e., illusory, temporal, ephemeral, transitory, ever-changing, that they should be renounced. Instead, the pretense of owning persists, the facade of possession gets acted out, and the vacant dream of vaunted satisfaction rolls on interminably. The compelling desire is for attaining that impossible Utopian Society. Herein comes the final teaching on the chart on page 11.

Displayed in the box on the lower right hand corner of the chart are two of the most precious teachings on objects ever given. Both of the teaching points are divided into two parts. Teaching number one is that all objects are empty. Teaching number two is that all objects are mental projections. When these two teachings are taken side by side and contemplated over time, the initial disappointment at finding the world to be insubstantial transforms into the gradual, then abiding, elation of freedom. Here is how that process works:

In the Ishavasyopanisad, in its very first sloka, the point is made that *"one is not to covet the goods or wealth of other beings."*

Classical Yoga concurs with this, since it has as one of its initial tenets the *yama* of *asteya*, nonstealing/noncoveting. The ideology around this gets expressed thusly: *"Whatever there is that is changeful in this ephemeral world, all of that must be enveloped by the Lord. By this renunciation should you support yourself."* Far from being a statement on moral rectitude alone, the main point comes through that the world is ephemeral, and is to be renounced. One "gets the Lord" by such renunciation.

The Elation of Renunciation

In Tantra's deep play with the teaching of Sankhya Yoga's twenty-four Cosmic Principles, all that has to do with the physical level of existence is categorized under an overall heading termed *nivritti* – to be renounced. This is not a teaching to be contemplated, like the axioms of Advaita for instance; this renunciation is obvious, practical, and a matter of course. The world is to be summarily given up, even and especially, while one is in it and occupying a physical body.

Vedanta states, *"Brahman Satya, Jagad Mithya – God is real, the world is unreal."* It is therefore that Sri Ramakrishna Paramahamsa declares that *"Man is born to no purpose when, having been given the boon of a human body, he is unable to realize God in this very life."* Whether this noble truth is expressed by way of philosophy, or via the convincing words of an *Avatara*, the accomplishment of said renunciation is paramount and, somewhat ironically, key to living a real life, a dharmic life, a God-centered life, or as Jesus put it, an Eternal Life.

The elation of giving up is what gives spiritual life its divine attraction. Weak souls will not feel it, will not get attracted, but strong souls will rush into its welcome embrace. But long before such surrender is achieved by resilient souls, some grand convincing, philosophically speaking, will need to be effected.

The first teaching on the chart on page 11 insists that objects are empty, and that has been demonstrated clearly enough thus far. Further reasoning is given, however, that objects are not just empty of real substance, but also of the ability to fulfill. This statement strikes closer to home with regard to people's comfort zones, those areas of covetousness that the scriptures have always spoken to and against. Therefore, if we look at the object of desire, and the human being's actions with regard to it, it becomes obvious that a certain mode of heedlessness is present in the mind when the mind is present with the object. To be more specific, the human relationship with the object over long sweeps of time has always been one of attachment and dependence, and seldom one of detachment and transcendence. In other words, the soul courts the demise of its own spirituality when it fastens to objects.

If the soul were to inspect its many-lifetime relationship with the objects of this world, it would see that objects decay and break. They also get lost or stolen. Further, they become boring and uninteresting. Finally, they only take up space and collect dust. In the end, it becomes a bother to divest oneself of possessions, and if one fails to do so, an accumulation builds up, causing the mind to brood, worry, and feel weighed down.

Add to all of this the fact that, over periods of time spent with objects, never has the mind experienced any lasting satisfaction in accord with them. As the Paramahamsa has also stated in this regard, *"Once a sweetmeat has gone down the throat, it and its taste are forgotten seconds later."* To quote an old saying, "Satiation never comes." And when it is attempted, the result is the inevitable wearing out of the physical organs. Disease is the eventual result of this. The mind, then, never gains the peace that it is really seeking in and throughout its relationship with the world and its objects. In telling fashion, the next sloka of the *Ishavasyopanisad* declares: *"Never by coveting, but only by performing scripturally ordained works, should one desire to live a life of a hundred years. In no other way can one be free of the taint of evil deeds so long as one is attached to human life in the body."*

Eternity Cannot be Lost

The predicament of mankind is that he projects the universes in time and space by conceiving name and congealing form with his own mental faculty and facility. But by the time he enters into the picture, called embodiment via the womb, he has forgotten both how and that he did it. And once he enters the field of his own projection, and begins to seek things/objects that really already belong to him, he tries to own and covet them, and even strives to amass these empty conjurings of his own mind. Then, when he fails, and loses them, he plunges himself into disparity and depression. In other words, he produces everything, even his own body, prior to embodiment, then moves amidst the projected world seeking objects of his own manufacture, loses them, and thinks that they are gone forever.

But eternity cannot be lost. To solve all his dilemmas he will have to slow down the speed with which the mind moves so he can uncover the ruse he is perpetrating on himself with his own ego/mind mechanism. Meditation is the excellent method with which to accomplish this. It is like slowing down a movie so as to see each frame as it goes by — not in a series of indeterminable flashes that are too quick to comprehend, but in a gradual way that allows for the *Dissolution of the Mindstream*.

The second teaching in the box on the chart on page 11 speaks to a different area of the human thinking process, and takes up a different trajectory and psychology as well. The seers have found out that the universe is just mind made manifest, that objects are only thought concretized via the power of mental vibration. The fourfold ego/mind/intelligence/thought mechanism, called the *Antahkarana* — "The Inner Cause" — is by its very nature a congealer and dissolver of name and form.

Given the imminence of this inherent power of mind, the rapt thinker will come to two beneficial conclusions with regard to Existence. First, all the primal doubt and fear around the Ultimate Existence of a Void will be defeated, i.e., one will be able to effectively "avoid the Void." Entertaining erroneous thoughts around the prospect of Nihilism can thus be annihilated, all based upon the knowledge that "nothing does not exist."

Put in another way, when the newborn seer perceives that it is the mind that is producing and withdrawing the universe in time and space, that insight lets God, Divine Reality, out of the creative equation. India has always known that God is "acreate" anyway. This realization will allow the mind to approach Reality as the Formless Essence that It is, and to avoid errant overlays and sublations that really belong to the realm of maya/nature, and not to God. As Sri Krishna puts it in the Bhagavad Gita: *"The Lord does not create agency or actions for the world; He does not create union with the fruits of action. Nature does all this. The Omnipresent does not take note of the merit and demerit of any. Knowledge is veiled by ignorance; mortals are thereby deluded."*

To conclude the subject, all objects and bodies, whether they be physical, heavenly, or conceptual, are neither created by God, nor are they conjured up out of nothing. This leaves the agnostic and the nihilist nowhere to hide. And who would want to run away from the Truth anyway? It is only left to each one to figure out, individually, how to refrain from futile and negative mental projections and, becoming pure again, begin to contribute to mankind's search for ultimate and abiding freedom.

For, whether one believes or disbelieves in Divine Reality, or even holds no opinion on the subject whatsoever, the reality of human suffering does not go away. It is everyone's business. The sensible person is the sensitive person, and sincere well-wishers will not ignore such problems and just walk away. All levels of human awareness are to be inspected, conquered, and utilized for the highest good of living beings. It is just that such superlative benefit cannot manifest in the mind that is clouded by root ignorance, dimmed by cluelessness around the illusory nature of objects, and verily darkened thereby and thereafter by unwholesome root evils such as lust, anger, covetousness, greed, and other base influences that are alien to the original Mind.

It is this root ignorance, called *avidya*, or *mulavidya*, that is to be taken up next for study. This study will reveal to the human mind its primal error in projecting unreal superimpositions over Primeval Awareness. As Sri Krishna states in the Bhagavad Gita, *"The unreal never is; the Real never ceases to be. The truth about both of these has been known by the seers."*

Chapter Two

Curtain of Nescience, Cloud of Unknowing

A crucial part of the ability to dissolve the mindstream involves coming to grips with the infamous *Curtain of Nescience*, scarcely mentioned (and even then with bated breath) even in spiritual circles where concerned acharyas seek only the unconditional freedom of their precious disciples. A main stumbling block here is the overall scarcity of information about this subtle obstacle in consciousness. Most beings never surmise that their awareness even holds boundless wisdom and bliss — the entire projection of the Cosmic Mind — within it, what to speak of suspecting that there is a subtle superimposition lying over it. In order to find it and penetrate it, it will be necessary to locate its hiding place, which is intricately tucked into the primal root ignorance of the human mind.

Associated in scriptures with the third state of human awareness called *Sushupti,* deep sleep, the Curtain of Nescience is a veil of cosmic proportions that naturally attends upon and obscures consciousness from the deeper vision of subtle truths that lie within its own vibrational territories. Thus, Sanskrit words such as *maya, avidya, avarana, adhyasa, vivarta* and others, also find close correspondence with it. The student might well comprehend, then, why a study of the *Deva-Bhasha*, the Language of the Gods, must be a natural embellishment to spiritual life, simply because there are words for such hidden but important principles in Sanskrit (*Arsha-Bhasha*). The ancient rishis of India found all things in consciousness — some of them being of the very nature of obscurity — and astutely identified them with key words and phrases.

≈CURTAIN OF NESCIENCE/CLOUD OF UNKNOWING≈

"When mentation, with all its facets and emanations, is engaged in devoid of full awareness, stripped of the knowledge of the Self within, then the universe in space and time rises out of nescience, root ignorance. But, if the true nature of all things is known prior to embodiment in the three worlds, the entire affair becomes nothing other than Brahman." — Lord Vasishtha

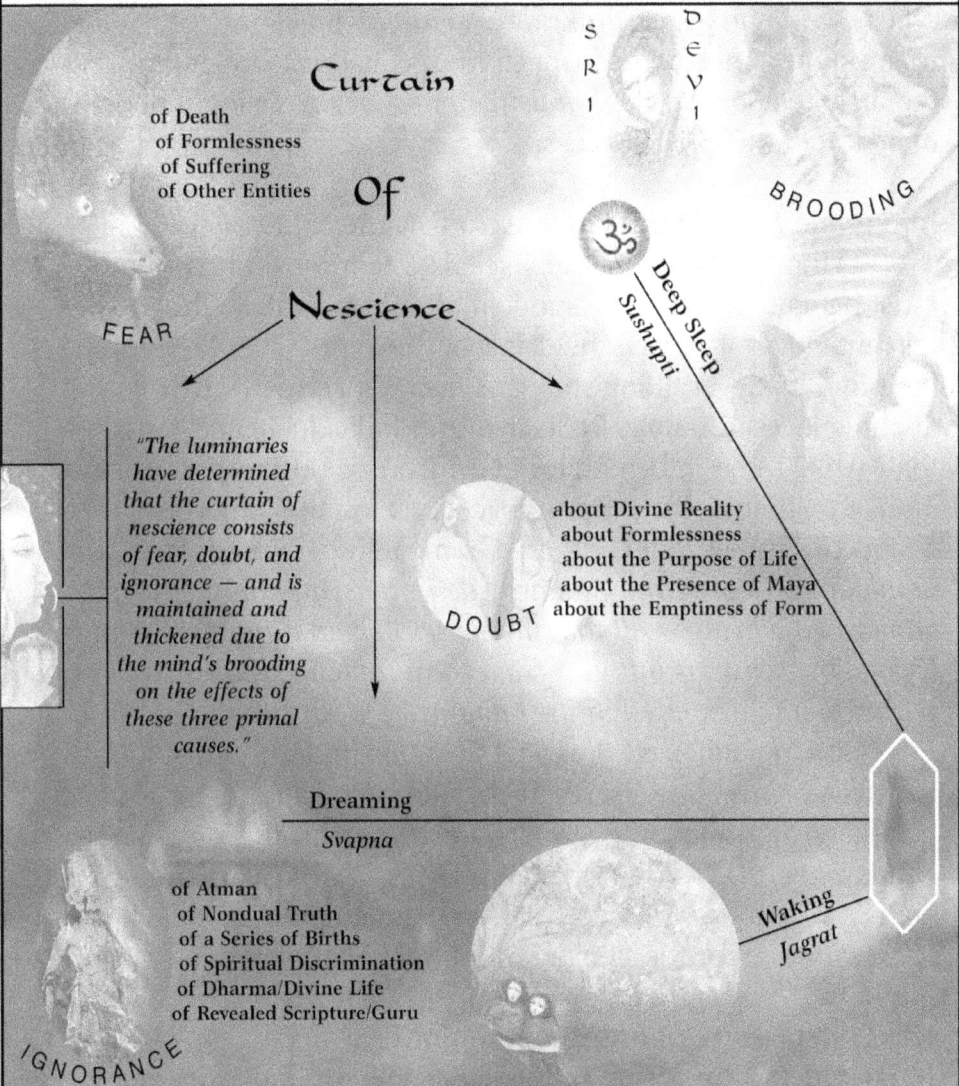

Curtain
of Death
of Formlessness
of Suffering
of Other Entities

Of

SRI DEVI

BROODING

Deep Sleep / Sushupti

Nescience

FEAR

"The luminaries have determined that the curtain of nescience consists of fear, doubt, and ignorance — and is maintained and thickened due to the mind's brooding on the effects of these three primal causes."

DOUBT
about Divine Reality
about Formlessness
about the Purpose of Life
about the Presence of Maya
about the Emptiness of Form

Dreaming / Svapna

of Atman
of Nondual Truth
of a Series of Births
of Spiritual Discrimination
of Dharma/Divine Life
of Revealed Scripture/Guru

Waking / Jagrat

IGNORANCE

"As Ram listened carefully, Lord Vasishtha spoke of Uddalaka's piercing of the curtain of nescience: 'Mere wisps of thoughts occurred to his mind, but he dissolved them on the spot. When the subtle tendency towards vikalpa arose, he quelled that immediately. Soon, even the darkness that gathered, indicative of primal ignorance, was overcome by his nondual mental stance, and he came upon and beheld a Great Light. Amazed, he pierced through it as well, along with the dizziness which came from gazing upon it. Thus, the stage of darkness and light was transcended.'" — Yoga Vasishtha

Chart by Babaji Bob Kindler — Property of SRV Associations

But this cosmic mask of maya, sometimes aptly referred to as the "Cloud of Unknowing," has many more implications than inscrutable obscuring power. It is also the boundless and elastic shell and container of all that lies within the infinite properties of unmanifested *Prakriti*. An intellectual study of it, what to speak of a meditative inspection of it, is therefore essential to the art of *Dissolving the Mindstream*, as well as being a penultimate level to its final success.

Intangible Matter: the Unconscious Material Energy

Unmanifested Prakriti, itself, is a flummoxing concept for most beings. Defined as "subtle matter in potential," the greater percentage of it always held in abeyance, it will suffice to say here that it is everything that was ever conceived of by mind at its three levels (Cosmic, Collective, and Individual), and far more than what came into manifestation from it on the earth plane. Thinking in this way, the implications of the timeless Peace chants of Mother India find greater meaning: *"Purnamadah purnamidam purnat purna mudachyate purnasya punamidaya purnameva vasishyate – All that the senses behold is finite; all that is beyond the senses is infinite. From the infinite the finite has come, yet being infinite, only infinite remains."*

If Unmanifested Prakriti, the subtle material substance of the universes, is so vast, then the rare and intrepid soul once beholding it could only stand back in awe at the diaphanous wrapping surrounding it. Penetrating it for the sake of gaining higher Awareness will be a very ambitious undertaking, albeit a necessary one for the attainment of full Enlightenment.

The Constituents of Spiritual Blindness

Due to the nature of nescience, the aspirant after spiritual freedom might conclude that penetrating it is an impossible task, or at the very least an undertaking devoid of any guidebook or training manual. For, the scriptures seldom mention such a principle, perhaps knowing that, for the average human being turned seeker, it will be enough to just locate and remove the basic human passions and foibles from the mind's interior. But this is precisely the point.

As our chart on page 19 aptly demonstrates, the Curtain of Nescience actually consists of just such shortcomings and inconsistencies. The more confusing problem is really that there is a mass of them, and they have accumulated over many lifetimes. Here comes the curtain's inscrutable connection with the relative laws of karma and reincarnation, what to speak of *samskaras,* those pesky mental complexes that were also constructed in the mind's fabric over a succession of many births and deaths, all of this unbeknownst to most embodied beings.

For the sake of ease of comprehension, and so to more readily initiate a plan of action around thinning this otherwise impermeable curtain over consciousness, the mass of transgressions and ignorant thoughts and acts that pepper the recesses of it can be categorized into three main areas: they are fear, doubt, and ignorance. To repeat the saying of Lord Siva shown on the chart under study (page 19), *"The luminaries have determined that the curtain of nescience consists of fear, doubt, and ignorance – and it is maintained and thickened due to the mind's brooding on the effects of these three primal causes."*

The daunted spiritual seeker may breathe a sigh of relief upon receiving this welcome teaching, but the optimistic spiritual aspirant will go forward straight away and begin thinning out the curtain by giving up all manner of brooding on the mind's admixture of various considerations.

At this point one can clearly see the import of these direct beneficial inward actions, or sadhana, in the scope of practicing the *Dissolution of the Mindstream.* For, what is it that perplexes beings more than their own minds? The mind contains an amalgam of the six passions, the eight fetters, the ego complex, the pool of thoughts, and the intellectual sheath – but this is all connected to morality and cosmology. Additionally, the practitioner now finds that there are primal causes involved in the mind's processes as well, and they are not so hidden and subtle as they were originally thought to be. Only, this melange of ingredients are ages-old, maybe even timeless, which brings up another helpful hint for the thinning process to come.

Both the *Dissolution of the Mindstream* practice and the thinning of the Curtain of Nescience are to be accomplished and dealt with based on the axiom of *Advaita Vedanta,* or Nonduality. No practice or problem should ever be entered into by the adept practitioner without first proclaiming and affirming that the Soul, the Self of mankind, Atman, is pure and perfect to begin with, beyond beginnings.

The threefold constituents of the Curtain of Nescience are to be looked at in this halcyon light. If the initial dissolution practice and its study have revealed the ultimately unreal nature of the elements and senses, along with the fourfold mind, then how real can fear, doubt, and ignorance be, since they are all contained in that selfsame mind? The "no head, no headache" psychology applies here, or, to put it another way, the one thousand year old darkness in a newly discovered cave takes only seconds to disperse once the explorer enters with a torch.

The fear, doubt, and ignorance package, then, is not so daunting as it seems. Day to day practice based upon their discovery, and the knowledge of their transparency, will be enough to make holes in said curtain — blissful apertures that will both allow penetration beyond the causal body and its infatuation with Unmanifested Prakriti, as well as introduce the guiding Light of Brahman to provide for full access — Samadhi.

Meditation and the Impure Mind

As for thinning out the Curtain of Nescience so that this access can be gained, a deep scrutiny of the recesses of the mind is duly advised by the luminaries. Here is where *Dissolving the Mindstream* as a preferred technique reveals both its superiority and its main difficulty. Preparedness, or lack thereof, is the defining qualifier.

Meditation as a practice, in general, has always been advised by the seers. However, and as the stunted condition of today's contemporary practitioners has proven, meditation on its own, before the mind is sufficiently purified, is ineffective as a means to Enlightenment, and often only leads the novice and intermediate alike into overall uncertainty. And what to speak of external or internal actions, the great Souls of the world warn against entering into any of the finer practices of spiritual life without first having attained purification of body, senses, and mind. To do an act — anything from moving outside of one's house, to sitting for daily meditation — is ideally only to be done in a balanced state of mind. Otherwise, mixed and negative ramifications are bound to rise and circulate.

To focus in on the subject of meditation specifically, the rare teaching comes that it is not a good tool for purification. The uninformed, both teachers and practitioners, have been using it for that, and for health, healing, psychic purposes, even the gaining of visions for the sake of gaining visions, for generations. However, *jnana*, knowledge, is the purifier for the mind; *bhakti*, devotion, is the purifier for the heart/emotions. Finally, *karma yoga*, if rightly utilized, is the purifier of actions. With all three of these in place, meditation finds its true facility as well — as the meeting place between God and devotee.

Dissolving the Mindstream, then, is meditation in action, not in the area of external action, but in the realm of internal action. Thus, it is a form of jnana. To finally see all that lies within the mind, i.e., *"the kingdoms of heaven,"* suits a twofold purpose. First, it shows the soul its field — the *"fields of the Lord."* Secondly, it reveals the crucial distinction between Insentient Matter *(Prakriti)* and Sentient Spirit *(Purusha)*. The soul can easily forego the former and take up the latter once the vision of Reality is glimpsed. The Curtain of Nescience thins of itself whenever Divine Reality makes an appearance. Spirituality destroys ignorance on the spot, proving to the aspirant the Vedantic axiom that *"Brahman is Real and the world is unreal."* In That Light, fear is made afraid of itself, doubt is caused to doubt itself, and ignorance is rendered ignorant of itself. Death is placed in its own grave. Then, from the cradle to the grave, mankind will not live in nescience anymore.

To put a finer and more streamlined point on this, practice of the *Dissolution of the Mindstream IS* purification — not of the external or moral kind, but of the dharmic kind. One does not give up smoking and drinking, adopt good habits around cleansing the body, become a vegetarian, refrain from swearing, and initiate other efforts of that ilk, then go to sit in meditation thinking that essential purification has been accomplished. What about all the residues of numerous acts and thoughts committed in past lifetimes that still reside in the mind? Will a few moral exercises get rid of them?

To repeat, an in-depth scrutiny of the deep recesses of the mind is required, along with the sure and certain follow up of bringing the power of dissolution to bear upon these dark areas. The experienced adept will discover that the practice of meditation after such inner work has been completed is an entirely illuminating experience. A thousand mistakes and miscues will be avoided in this way, and the crucial seventh limb of Yoga, i.e., meditation, will offer up its inmost treasures.

Thinning the Curtain of Nescience

With the help of the chart still under study on page 19, some more guidance in the process of the eradication of errant thoughts and antiquated concepts can be offered.

As with anything associated with spirituality — its tenets, its practice, its difficulties, its attainment — there is no comparison between it and worldly endeavors. The soul is headed in an entirely opposite direction when authentic spiritual life is taken up. That is why the illumined preceptors insist upon full commitment first, followed by an all-out effort to attain the Ideal thereafter. Failure to conclude this ultimate quest, once taken up, is a serious mistake, for the luminaries have seen that giving up develops a habit of failure in the mind that worsens over time with all further belated attempts.

"Changing horses in the middle of the stream" in order to get spiritual experiences from a "more desirable" teacher is another common mistake of the novitiate practitioner, what Zen calls *Hasan*. It is an interruption of one's practice in favor of sensational pursuits. On the contrary, it is *Isshi-injo* that is wanted, deep and long-standing training under one preceptor in order to get *Ishin-denshin*, the direct transmission of what one's chosen teacher has realized. Otherwise the student starts showing signs of *Yako Zen*, the "Wild Fox Zen," and pretends to be spiritual while only doing lip service to the teachings. By this time, any appreciable spiritual progress is already spoiled.

Real progress, as far as the dissolution process is concerned, has to do with finding and facing off with the mind's inner obstacles *(vighna)*. In general, as has been said, these are fear, doubt, and ignorance around the true nature of things. Taking fear first, the chart on page 19 gives four aspects of fear most commonly found to be unresolved in the human mind. Importantly, the everyday fears that may or may not get treated by proper upbringing, schooling, therapy, and the like, is not what is being referred to here. These should have already been destroyed previously by every seeker who has entered into sincere commitment to the spiritual path.

The Illusion of Death

Fear of death, for instance, may be assuaged for a short time via some friendly advice from a worldly person or professional, but both the imminence of death on the mortal level, and the actual illusion of death on the spiritual level, are left unaddressed and unanswered. Only those who have seen, encountered, and conquered death based upon direct spiritual experience are qualified to address such a quandary. No one else can do so. The seer who is also an *acharya* (spiritual teacher of the revealed scriptures) has penetrated into such mysteries, having no karma to answer for and thus no fear of undue reprisals. Such a soul can walk into the realm of death and tell Yama, the Lord of Death: *"I have received a command from the Divine Mother of the Universe that death must die!"* The Lord of Death bows to such a being, and hastily retreats.

The second entry on the chart in the fear category is the

reason why the seer can perform such rare and unconventional acts of courage, i.e., fear of formlessness has been transcended as well. Formlessness is quite deathlike. In reality it is the death of the ego, the "unreal" and "empty" self, that is meant here. It is a matter of great interest to the inwardly aspiring seeker after Truth that the ego mechanism disappears during deep sleep. Where has it gone? he queries; how has it returned?

The answer, at least for the ordinary seeker, is connected to the Curtain of Nescience. The consciousness of a human being dissolves into that simulacrum of real formlessness at the time of deep sleep and, probably also at the time of death — unless meditation practice during one's life has effectively dissipated it. The more glimpses of Divine Reality that can be had during the span of one's embodied state, the more likelihood there will be of the descent of insights and revelations that are so profound that ignorance will have no choice but to expire.

To conclude on the presence of the fear of formlessness, the only real solution is to enter into it; but this must be attempted only after the dissolution of all physical and subtle principles, i.e., the elements, senses, and mind complex, has been attained, thus known (to be unreal), and mastered. The causal level of man's awareness is soporific, that is, its influence tends to dull awareness rather than awaken it. Only masters of Awareness can enter into its obfuscating atmosphere, perceive its nature, and emerge with higher consciousness intact. This is where the *Ajna Chakra* is important, the awakening of Consciousness at the level of the sixth center, called the "Third Eye."

Fear of suffering is another difficult barrier to be conquered. Teachings like the Six Transformations — birth, growth, disease, old age, decay, and death — help in its mastery; also, the Four Noble Truths of Buddhism. Knowledge of the mind's ability to first forebear suffering, then to transcend it completely, also benefits the seeker. What is not helpful is belief in the ultimate reality of suffering. Forbearance is not fatality. Putting up with suffering only so long as it takes to gain and experience higher spiritual stations, like wisdom and bliss, is what is wanted.

Trepidation around the presence and actions of other entities concludes the list under the heading of fear. Certainly, the Curtain of Nescience expands and contracts exponentially in proportion to the quality of thoughts that pass through the mind daily. Negative vibrations, what the Father of Yoga calls *klistha vrittis*, add hefty weight to the wall of ignorance that then comes falling down over the mind of the brooding individual. To keep the mind ever buoyant, like a hot air balloon, is advised by the sages and seers. To thicken the Cloud of Unknowing with even more clouds is to deludedly *"....pile more gloom on gloom,"* as Swami Vivekananda has written.

Since collective consciousness is an indeterminable and unpredictable mass of chaotic and volatile vibrational admixtures, the spiritual aspirant learns to keep a healthy distance from beings who live in and permit such undesirable occupations as anger, resentment, violence, and hatred. Soon, with such careful procedures adhered to, a natural protection – a different type of curtain – surrounds the aspirant, and he or she is spontaneously led away from all harm and into pathways which lead only to Light. This is sometimes called "Grace," and every spiritual luminary attests to its salubrious presence.

The Unholy Matrimony of Doubt and Ignorance

The other two ingredients of the Curtain of Nescience are doubt and ignorance. By referring again to the chart under study on page 19, the reader can see the dynamics of how these two work, both individually and in tandem.

The list under the heading of doubt represents most of the main impediments at all levels of existence, and ones that most seekers – whether they be seekers after worldly aims or seekers of spiritual ends – have encountered. The sequence is also rather telling. That is, if the soul comes into the embodied condition holding any doubt about the existence or nature of Divine Reality, there will be hell to pay.

First, with no knowledge of the truth of formlessness, and thereby no seeking of anything beyond the realms of name and form, the soul falls into complacency about the true meaning of life and comes under Maya's influence without even knowing it. Since Maya is the realm of name and form, that is all the soul will seek, and it will begin to think only in terms of the gross nature of things.

But, to quote the Diamond Sutra, *"Form is emptiness and emptiness is form"*; no real satisfaction can be gained until form is perceived to be empty of substance and empty of the ability to fulfill. Otherwise, the element of doubt residing in the Curtain of Nescience incapacitates the soul, leaving it both listless and helpless in the end.

Ignorance may be the cause for doubt, but an equally strong case can be made that doubt infuses ignorance and lends it further power, much like the combination of obscuration and distortion. In the case of ignorance, however, its very existence is primal. Such is its power of pervasiveness that it will persist even long after initial spiritual awakening has taken place, as is instanced by the fact that so many souls fall back into nescience after a short stint in the realm of spiritual disciplines.

Yet, it is spiritual discipline, sadhana, that removes ignorance, avidya. Case in point, is that three strong components of sadhana are found in the list on page 19 under the heading of ignorance, namely, *viveka, dharma,* and *vidya-shastra.* Spiritual discrimination, wisdom teachings, and the testament of the seers via revealed scriptures form a winning combination — a sort of one-two-three punch that will, if cultivated constantly, put ignorance to the mat once and for all.

And as the list on the chart under study (page 19) further reveals, the lack of this intense and well-guided practice will veil another key element in the process of spiritual awakening, that being the series of lifetimes that the soul has assumed — all of them, up to this point in the current of time, lived in ignorance. Ignorance of one's true nature as Atman, and the failure to maintain adherence to Nondual Truth, robs the embodied soul of the main powers that he or she will need for living a dharmic life on earth, what to speak of gaining Enlightenment there.

Curtain of Nescience 29

With this basic rundown of the deterring forces contained in the Curtain of Nescience completed, the meditator who is interested primarily in achieving swift success in *Dissolving the Mindstream* has to look at the mind's tendency to brood. Just like the changing conditions of weather duly thicken the presence of a fogbank, so too does the habit of brooding thicken the Curtain of Nescience.

Again, if the soul were to know for certain that the world is unreal, that objects cannot fulfill, that only one's own efforts can bring freedom, that Reality is neither matter, energy, or a thought form, then the habit of brooding would never gain a foothold in the mind in the first place.

This brooks another problem: that our children are not taught these truths early on in life, before they seek to master the mind, either consciously or unconsciously. Instead, they are sent headlong into the vexing fray of unreal and empty objects, fruitless actions, misguided undertakings, and pointless relationships, devoid of any discriminating wisdom. It is fortunate, indeed, when a young man or woman finds their way to an enlightened soul prior to entering into the world and what it promises. Provided that such a youth has not become jaded early on via poor upbringing by worldly parents, fundamentalist religion, and a wealth and fame-oriented society, a chance to hear the Truth will save him or her from certain death in ignorance. Of course, it is spirituality that dies here, not the Supreme Soul. Nevertheless, and as Kamalakanta sings about life in the world in one of his wisdom songs: *"Suffering will come, even if one seeks the Truth. But how many more lifetimes in ignorance can I bear?"*

The useless act of brooding, like so many other habits, is exceedingly hard to break once it has settled in. And as those under its influence can attest to, there are a host of things to brood upon in this life. The Tantras call this by the name, *shatavadana* – "thinking of a thousand things at once." It fits well with another related tendency called *vaichitra*, "varieties." To think constantly in obsessive fashion on a multitude of considerations is to both riddle the mind with nervous passageways, as well as to take away its right and ability to concentrate on Divine Reality first and foremost. The sacred rule in this regard is to *"Seek thee first the Kingdom of Heaven"* so that *"....all will be added unto thee."* Alas, when no clear and salient teachings have ever been given to the soul about the Kingdom of Heaven, how will it ever come to seek it, what to speak of recognizing it when it occasionally presents itself on earth in the form of *guru, dharma,* and *sangha?* The predicament here is obvious, and the end result is gravely unfortunate.

The Ills of Desire-Based Mental Projection

To render more lucidity to the problem of brooding, the chart on the facing page outlines many of the modes of projection that plague the embodied soul, all placed in three categories. This teaching is mainly a gift of Lord Vasishtha, and it plays off of another teaching given by Sri Krishna in the *Bhagavad Gita*. It utilizes the relative principles of *sankalpa* and *vikalpa*, which are cautionary words that indicate reckless and random mental projection devoid of any higher design or desire.

Sankalpa is a real problem, mainly because it is so often utilized only in the realm of base desire. It is in this context that Sri Krishna tells Arjuna, *"Sankalpa is a positive evil. Renounce it."* Whereas many beings may assess life in the world to be a good and positive thing, the more experienced soul has seen through the surface appearances and noted the underlying presence of suffering in everything. The great and brutal war on the battlefield of Kurukshetra, upon which the above advice is given, is a fitting place to get this point across to an awakening soul. War, any war, represents the clashing and intermingling of hosts of karmas — individual, collective, and cosmic — all of which are precisely aligned with the three levels of mental projection shown on the chart on page 31.

Pleasure and dominion over the physical world, anticipation for more of the same in the celestial spheres, and the desire for power over others based in pride and glory, make up the

The Three Levels of Sankalpa/Vikalpa

"Sankalpic desire at three levels — the world, the mind, and the intellect — when utilized by an unillumined mind is a detrimental force at the root of all suffering. It is like a rutting elephant whose trunk is the tendency of selfish grasping and who goes about spraying the world with the water of surface enjoyments. Only the sharp arrow of Atmajnan can bring this lumbering beast to its knees so it can be bound by the ropes of masterful mind control."   Lord Vasishtha

Lord Vasishtha

1. The World:
Desire for Physical Objects

for foods, for sense objects, for pleasures, for possessions

2. The Mind:
Desire for Mental Projection

for worlds, for heavens, for excitements, for distractions

3. The Intellect:
Desire for Attainments

for power, for manipulation, for pride, for glory

Mental Modes

Hoping for

Brooding upon

Seeking after

Owning

Coveting

Enjoying

Striving for

Accumulating

Clinging to

Nonsharing

Taking as real

Conceiving

Thinking on

Imagining

Creating

Projecting

Fantasizing about

"For mastery over sankalpa and vikalpa practice asamvedana — nonreceptivity to all desire. Instead of falling in love with your own desires as if they were fulfilling, you must instead begin to perceive them as burdens, like packages and parcels filled with unwanted items that really clutter your life and only weigh you down."   Lord Vasishtha in Yoga Vasishtha

Chart by Babaji Bob Kindler   Property of SRV Associates

three levels of sankalpa/vikalpa. As stations of consciousness, these three and their respective locations correspond to the world, the mind, and the intellect. The modes around which the mind revolves in this three-leveled process are legion, as listed on the chart. Everything from the aforementioned problem of brooding, to obvious negativities like covetousness and selfishness, to the questionable occupations of hope, fantasizing, and imagination, to the habitual preoccupations of ownership, pleasure, and attachment, and on through to the seemingly positive actions of seeking, striving, creating, and thinking – it is all classed under the heading of mental conjuring.

When this list of sankalpic emanations is noted under the three headings on the sidebar of the chart, the aspirant after freedom suddenly sees and understands both the power of the mind to fashion all manner of worlds, objects, and relationships, as well as its tendency to bind itself inextricably into the same.

Another way of bringing such an unconventional teaching and perspective forward, and impressing it on the soul, is to point out the lack of peace of mind that so many beings under the influence of sankalpa and vikalpa suffer from. Not only is there no equanimity in such a mind, but the inability to simply be still, calm, or quiet disappears. This is *Kshipta*, habitually scattered mind, accompanied in turns by *mudha*, dull mind. Living in these two modes, with no break, the mental apparatus gets damaged, maybe for lifetimes, and rebirth in the human form becomes a very undesirable proposition. At best, in such a predicament, beings are born beset by shallowness, superficiality, and lack of intelligence. At worst, minds imbued with retardation, insanity, and habitual violence come forth. Thus, suffering is born along with the body – and it spreads.

A Further Unwrapping of Sankalpa

It would be unfair to leave the reader with only this bare mention of the admittedly fascinating, albeit dangerous, mental process called sankalpa, especially since it is at the root of everything that the meditator is striving to dissolve.

Glimpsed in deep meditation by the ancient seers, and thereafter given a word, it was brought forward as a pat answer to questions that theretofore and even for centuries afterwards, plagued the thinking process of mankind. That God created the universe, or that it came about out of nothingness, or that matter was the source, or that intelligence developed in and after it — these are some of the untenable assumptions that got postulated by everyone from the priest class to the presiding intelligencia throughout phases of time. As Swami Vivekananda stated when he came to the West in the late 1800's:

"*Sober minded beings have become disgusted with their superstitious religions and are looking forward to India for new light. How eagerly they take in any little bit of the grand thoughts of the holy Vedas, which resist and are unharmed by the terrible onslaughts of modern science. The theories of creation out of nothing, or a created soul, and of the big tyrant of a God sitting on a throne in a place called heaven, and of eternal hell-fires, have disgusted all the educated; and the noble thoughts of the Vedas about the eternity of creation and of the soul, they are imbibing fast in one shape or another. Within fifty years the educated world will come to believe in the eternity of both soul and creation, and in God as our highest and perfect nature, as taught in our holy Vedas. Even now their learned priests are interpreting the Bible that way.*"

The chart on page 31 reads the riot act on mental projection, calling it out and designating it for what it is — an unholy pastime. For, sankalpa and vikalpa are modes of a dual mind that is firmly ensconced in the base habit of desire. If desire were not present, the projection of the mind would be both balanced and innocuous, ushering in only harmony and inherent knowledge of unity, rather than a host of base passions and fetters rooted in selfish grasping and inordinate attachment.

A case in point, is that the mental projection of the saints and seers is always *sattvic,* balanced, and taken on for the higher good of humanity, rather than a mere relative good for the self — and this latter often at the cost of suffering to others. It is in this vein — and to repeat — it is to enlighten the mind of Arjuna as to the reason for the presence of such things as war, violence, negative *karmas,* and the like, that Sri Krishna teaches in the Gita: *"Sankalpa is a positive evil, Arjuna. If one sees the mind engaging in it, one should swiftly and completely renounce it."* To quote Vivekananda on this selfsame subject, *"Peace of mind immediately follows such renunciation."*

Atmic Sankalpa and Mayic Sankalpa

The reader and student should know of the existence of positive sankalpa, called *Atmic Sankalpa.* Mayic sankalpa, the troublesome tendency of ceaseless mental vibration, is like a kind of internal chatter. It can be addressed and quelled. To give an example from the scriptures, the second verse of Patanjali's well-known *Yoga Sutras* states, *"Yogash chitta vritti nirodha,"* which translates into English as *"Union with Divine Reality is brought about by stilling the vibrations of the mind."* It is a different concept than what the conventional western mind is used to, for mental activity is generally considered a good pastime. Certainly, people are encouraged to think, so as to overcome slothfulness of mind. But this means positive thinking, not brooding, and certainly not harmful or evil thoughts.

Included in this purging process are thoughts that are both misdirected and indicative of potential fragmentation. A scattered mind is dangerous to itself and to others, its thoughts leading the individual to perpetrate all manner of ill-advised actions. The prisons of the world are full of many good people whose train of thoughts led them into the predicament they now find themselves in. Since *"....thought is father to the deed,"* the sincere seeker after self-control will delve into the source of thought in the human mind and render it neutral. This is both a necessity and a practicality, and it will demand a mental practice.

The Solution of the Thoughtless, "Nontouch" Yoga

To stop the incursion of such base ignorance and suffering, or to deter it before it even gets started, Lord Vasishtha recommends the singular practice of *Asamvedana*, mental transparency. The word is often defined as the "thoughtless state." meaning the possessor of it can quell the thoughts at any time under his or her own power and auspice.

The dynamics of asamvedana really revolve around non-receptivity to desire and its offspring. Instead of lingering on the railroad tracks of desire and attachment like the foolish person does, the freedom seeker puts an ear to them via meditation and perceives the distant vibration of the many approaching trains of karmas born of mindless longing and fantasizing over lifetimes. Then he simply stands up and moves off the tracks, out of the way of harm.

To become invisible to one's own limitations, then, is the unique way of the spiritual adept who is seeking *Dissolution of the Mindstream*. It follows the way of the path of least resistance, and also adheres to the words of the Christ when He said, *"Resist not evil."* Put in a very positive Buddhist way, the teaching relates, *"When focusing occurs, focus without objective; when stabilizing occurs, stabilize free of distractions; when shifting occurs, shift without grasping; when manifestations arise, experience them as Reality, and when liberation occurs, allow it to happen naturally."*

In this chapter, the very subtle problem of the Curtain of Nescience has been duly brought forward for consideration. Admittedly, it is encountered at a very advanced level of inward search under the auspice of the *Dissolution of the Mindstream* practice. Nevertheless, an early mention of it will benefit the meditator later on along the path of effective detachment and renunciation.

In the following chapter, and to help the seeker further, an actual study of the methods and modes of meditation will be taken up – a study and list that is comprehensive, but rarely taught, even in advanced spiritual circles.

Chapter Three

The Secret of Comprehensive Meditation

As the chart on the facing page demonstrates, there is more to meditation than what has been taught to date in the West. Even within India's vast contribution to the spiritual art of meditation, rarely is it taught to students in any comprehensive way. Perhaps this is because authentic teachers of meditation know that such inward practice cannot really be taught at all. The aspiring soul must venture into the subtle and causal realms on its own, and most often without any provision whatsoever for the journey. Still, what basics can be given, should be given, and the following multifaceted teaching is offered in that very light.

Meditation, as given by the ancient rishis, the seers of earliest meditation, has two forms: the first is with attributes, and the second is devoid of attributes. The chart is thus divided into two sections, the top section labeled "create realms," and the bottom titled the "acreate realm." In the former, there are a host of lokas or worlds peopled by billions of forms, and there are nearly as many powers for overseeing them all. Whether one calls these powers laws, energies, or deities, the plethora of them provides the meditator with a very rich basis for reflection. The benefit of this is the acquisition of all knowledge with regard to the creative process. The disadvantage is that the soul may linger far too long in such deliberations and perhaps never actually find the Formless Essence which is the underlying substratum for all form, all projection.

Under this double heading of the two forms of meditation fall eight types of meditation, divided four and four, equally. Gradated as well, the early types of meditation on form begin with what is known as the *pratika*, or symbol. We should make

Two Forms & Eight Main Types of Meditation

S A G U N A   B R A H M A N

(Create Realms)

1) Pratika-pratimadhyana — Meditation on Objects
"By meditation upon those objects which are most agreeable, the yogi's mind attains blissful equipoise."   Lord Patanjali

2) Sukshmadhyana — Meditation on Subtle Truths
"To come to know the methods for removing desire, and how best to worship the acharya, the seer studies those scriptures which treat Atmic Reality and point the way to Self-cognition." Lord Vasishtha

3) Vyakti-upasanadhyana — Meditation on God with Form
"For many it is best to think of God as possessed of qualities and having a form. This way their minds will become easily concentrated."
Swami Sivananda

4) Lila-dhyana — Meditation on the Avatar's Divine Play
"Lila as God, Lila as the deities, Lila as man, Lila as the universe; take delight in the Naralila." Sri Ramakrishna

P R O J E C T I O N

↑ Meditation with Form (Saguna Brahman) ↑
↓ Meditation beyond Form (Nirguna Brahman) ↓

N I R G U N A   B R A H M A N

(Acreate Realm)

5) Tailadharadhyana — Meditation on One-pointedness
"The powers of the mind should be concentrated and turned back upon itself to penetrate its innermost secrets." Swami Vivekananda

6) Svarupadhyana — Meditation on the Inner Self
"The Self is master of the self; who else can the master be? With the finite self subdued, one obtains the sublime refuge most difficult to achieve."
Lord Buddha

7) Brahmakaravrittidhyana — Meditation on Brahman
"Remain quiet, indifferent to the body, and by that one thought of Brahman, become one with Brahman — undivided." Shankaracharya

8) Layachintayadhyana — Meditation to Achieve Immersion
   a) Bhuta-layachintayadhyana - of the physical
   b) Antahkarana-layachintayadhyana - of the mental
   c) Omkara-layachintayadhyana - of the initial cause

"When the mind is completely absorbed in the Supreme Being — Brahman — the world of appearances vanishes." Shankaracharya

D I S S O L U T I O N

Chart by Babaji Bob Kindler   Property of SRV Associations

no mistake about it, the early peoples who gathered along the Indus River, who were probably very Tantric in their religious practices and perspectives, thought of and saw all objects as symbols for Reality. That is why worship on the physical level was instigated in the first place. In India, it was never a matter of worshiping decaying matter, or seeking out occult mysticism, but more of a focus upon finding the clues and links in matter that pointed towards the deeper reality. Thus the many allurements and attractions present in the world of matter never sidetracked the truth seeker of India for long. Authentic and sincere worship, not abject fear or bids for power, made certain of this fact.

We can see by the quote of Patanjali on the chart on the previous page that meditation on objects is not only going to provide clues about subtler states of awareness, but is also going to usher in the initial foundation for peace and bliss. As we have noted in the case of the *Dissolution of the Mindstream* practice, once objects are seen to be "empty" – both of abiding substance and of the ability to fulfill – they can be relinquished, renounced, and the freedom that comes from this separation from nature, from matter, brings elation. Therefore, the Father of Yoga also states that the yogi gets more bliss from giving away than from receiving, from lightening possessions rather than from amassing them. The yamas of *asteya and aparigraha* – freedom from undue gain – are based upon such insight and ability. As the scriptures declare, *"Wealth is no good. Reflect on this well. There is no happiness in it whatsoever. This is the Truth. For the wealthy, there is fear even from a son. Everywhere, this is the normal way of things."* Therefore, the West should abandon the *bhoga marga*, path of enjoyment, and take up the *jnana marga*, the path of wisdom. Then objects will pose no threat.

Samadhis of Wisdom, Bliss, and Egolessness

Once this grand freedom from coveting and brooding upon objects is attained, the next area of interest are the scriptures and the wisdom teachings that flow from them. Much more engaging than mere objects, the inward-moving aspirant also finds that the scriptures are much deeper than words and their intellectual understanding. They form a world all their own. Called *"samprajnata,"* or seeded realms, the germs of wisdom lying in the vast fields of the Tantras, Vedas, Upanisads, and other wisdom testaments, are more like pregnant fruits ready to explode with light.

At first, this discovery shocks the meditator, leaving him in a state of overwhelm at the prospect of so much lying within him. After a period of adjustment, however, the soul finds an innate ability to select bits and fragments of this wisdom bounty and concentrates on each of them specifically, leaving the rest alone for a time. By isolating a particle of wisdom for inspection, and splitting it with one's own power of concentration, an implosion of bliss occurs — the bliss of inner understanding. When enough of these implosions, as insights, are gathered together and combined, the result is the advent of wisdom samadhi. It prepares the way for even deeper levels of samadhi, such as the samadhi of Bliss *(sananda)*, and the Samadhi of the pure self *(sasmita)*. The entire collection of samadhis, then, are brought to bear by the art of *Sukshmadhyana*, meditation on subtle truths found in the revealed scriptures.

Mankind: God Walking Around on Two Legs

After powerful vibrations of scriptural truths are well meditated upon, it is time to take up the divine human form for concentration. *Vyakti-upasanadhyana* is the sacred way of saying meditation on God in the human form. Ordinary beings will not suffice as subjects at this highest level of inner inspection and devotion — not friends, parents, siblings, teachers, nor intellectuals — not unless they be enlightened, spiritually speaking. As Ramprasad Sen, the poet-saint of Bengal, sings: *"To hope for help from friends or family provides no profound solution. Don't you know that all are lost here? Everyone lives in pallid imitation of everyone else."*

Recognition of the mundane rounds of daily life, and the hosts of bound beings that participate in hypnotized fashion, even willingly, in this pointless charade, provides the sincere seeker with a powerful impetus to get out of such languorous cycles. For this, the added inspiration of a Chosen Ideal, an *Ishtam*, is helpful, if not necessary. As Swami Sivananda, a direct disciple of Sri Ramakrishna, declares, *"For many it is best to think of God as possessed of qualities and having a form."* This is *Saguna Brahman,* the otherwise formless God clothed in the five sheaths of body, prana, mind, intellect, and ego, for the sake of the truth-seeker and the devotee. The Lord sacrifices for the devotees in this way by taking on a form, which is a precarious situation, however one assumes it.

The point here is that most beings do not have the capacity or the training to approach God via the formless mode. As surprising as it seems, many do not even know that a transcendent Reality exists, much less that they may someday be able to perceive It — to merge in their own Essence. But even Jesus declared that *"....one gets to the Father through the Son."* The Divine Being is that perfect Son, an illumined soul. Even short of the knowledge of an Avatar's form, the meditator may take a seer, rishi, yogi, or guru, as the object of meditation. If objects offer up their secrets in rapt meditation, then how much more will a sentient, illumined soul do so. The expression, "God with form" finds not only its validation here, but its fullest meaning. And there are still more beauteous realms of this mode to come.

Lila-dhyana is the next "go-to" point for those fortunate souls who are drinking in the nectar of the *"Lotus Feet of the Blessed Lord and Divine Mother of the Universe."* It also may be the last outpost or satellite station of form before the formless Reality is breached and entered. In India, all the highest forms of God, like Sri Rama and Lord Krishna, have the AUM symbol imprinted on the palm of their hand, indicating that going beyond meditation on God in His highest aspects will lead the meditator to "The Word," the entrance to Formless Reality.

Tell Your Soul a Story

Lila-dhyan, meditating on the "sport" of the Lord, consists

of reading about the feats, escapades, challenges, and victories of the Lord while He is in the body. In all religions this form of thought is utilized, but rarely is it seen as a mode of meditation specifically. In Christianity, the art of Lila-dhyan takes on the form of recreating the Christ child, the manger, the three wise men, the inner aroma of frankincense and myrrh, and all the events of Jesus' life that took place up until the time of his body's death, and even after. The lives of other superlative illumined beings such as Sri Ramachandra, Sri Krishna, Chaitanya, Buddha, Moses, Mohammed, and more, have all been utilized for inspiring the inner lives of religious adherents throughout the ages.

However, Lila-dhyana is not just study of the cosmic personality and the actions of these superlative souls, but is also taking the time to meditate upon the events of their blessed lives. In meditation, the sincere practitioner should recreate the life and actions of these ideals in form and relive them in their own consciousness, lingering specifically on certain aspects that please and inspire.

Part of the dynamics of this practice is that time is cut down and away, the seeming reality of its linear flow undermined and replaced by the prevailing power of the immediate moment. Through this mode one eventually realizes the illusoriness of time or, put in another way, that all of time exists in the "Eternal Moment." This is also the true meaning of The Word. The advanced meditator pierces the covering over the subtle truth of timelessness when he or she approaches The Word via meditation on God's ecstatic sport of Consciousness.

"The Wisdom Scriptures Declare: Reality is Formless"

In the Nirguna realm of Nondual Awareness, only pure Consciousness exists. It IS Existence. Since there is only one eternal and all-pervasive mass of indivisible Light there, it is impossible of description and must be experienced. Precious words, the likes of *Brahman, Atman, Allah, All-Mighty Father, Tathagatagarbha, Prajnaparam, Satchitananda, Yahweh, Ahura Mazda,* and *the Great Spirit,* are all accepted and agreed upon indicators of the presence of this ultimately unnameable Reality. The superlative spiritual experience that comes from meditating on this Supreme Verity, namely, samadhi, satori, kaivalya, moksha, mukti, nirvikalpa, nirvana, asamprajnata, fana, ecstasy, beatific vision, etc., have been experienced by thousands of saints, seers, sages, and saviors of all the world's religious traditions from time out of mind. Since it is uniquely singular, descriptions of It, as well as instructions for attaining It, called practices and disciplines, are few of mention and far between as well. Nevertheless, four have been gathered here on the chart under study on page 35.

The first of these has been given a name by the seers that succinctly defines both its feel and its flow. Termed *Tailadharadhyana*, its appellation suggests the uniform flowing of refined oil from one container to another, without the slightest variance in shape and content. Thus, it is a very apt explanation of what happens to the soul when it gets into, or even close to, the state of nonduality. The relative, conditioned consciousness of the aspiring human mind joins itself with the pure and limitless Consciousness of the Atman.

The result of this is the initial phase of new conditioning, what Patanjali, the Father of Yoga, calls the generation of mental impressions of samadhi that replace the mind's old impressions. Old impressions could be of the nature of anything from memories of worldly life, to facets of religious life, on through to modes of self-effort focused on the attainment of freedom. Whatever the case may be, the singular impression of early samadhi experiences erode these complexes and take up residence in the mind in their place. This is what we see when we look at a luminary, despite all and other appearances.

Tailadharadhyana is both duly operated and effectively applied via mastery of concentration, what Vedanta calls *samadhana* — a special type of focus that allows only divine thoughts of God to enter into the interior of the mind. It is by thought on Reality alone, then, that samadhi dawns on the human mind, bringing some even subtler modes of formlessness to bear.

One of these is called *Svarupadhyana*. The Sanskrit word, *svarupa*, is reserved only for the highest implications, pointing directly to one's "essence." Here is where the soul learns to meditate on its own nature in order to close the door on all forms of duality, all thought of forms, too. As the Gita states about the yogi, *"He meditates on the Self, by the Self, in the Self, and becomes satisfied with the Self."* This Self is not to be confused with the ego-self; the Atman is not the *anatman*, obviously. Anatman is substanceless. Atman is fullness, purnayata. It is more like the profound term *Tathagatagarbha* in Buddhism, a primal, immovable, and eternal Station. It is unchanging Essence. The Buddha himself made the distinction between the two in the Dhammapada, stating: *"The Self is master of the self; who else can the master be? With the finite self subdued, one attains to that sublime refuge most difficult to achieve."*

Atman and Brahman

It is here that the student, what to speak of the rapt meditator, perceives the unity of Atman and Brahman. As spoken of earlier in this book, the Atman is a term for Reality, or Supreme Soul, who holds this one distinction from Brahman: It surrounds itself with coverings called sheaths, or *upadhis* (body, energy, mind, intellect, and ego). These five sheaths are used to express a bit of all that is in the Soul. If the embodied soul that is imbued with these five sheaths begins to identify with them, then it loses sight of its *svarupa*, its essence, and suffers ignorance and resultant suffering. It is in this way that the teaching of the slight distinction between Atman and Brahman is put forth, so as to explain the presence of maya and the unwise dive into cycles of birth and death in ignorance of the Truth — that the Soul is Formless.

This also makes sense out of the third level of formless meditation, called *Brahmakaravrittidhyana*. This august title infers that the initial cause *(kara)* of all vibration *(vritti)* has been eradicated, leaving only Brahman — Formless Reality — in the subtle wake of its outright disappearance. It is at this very sublime point that the full concentration, which was experienced in the state of Tailadharadhyana, turns into absorption. In other words, there is an approach to formless Reality, followed by a strong desire to merge in It, ending in all-out absorption into It. This sequence is better looked at by studying and reviewing the fourth and final description on the chart on page 37, which also brings in the return of the practice of *Dissolving the Mindstream*.

As Shankara states in his *Vivekachudamani*, *"When the mind gets completely absorbed in the Supreme Being, Brahman, the world of appearances vanishes."* According to the three phases of *Layachintayadhyana*, this meditation is undertaken for the express purpose of dissolving form completely. Since the point has been made that everything exists, that nothing has an ending, what to speak of a beginning, the mind is really only involved here with taking the acid-like nature of Consciousness in the form of focused intelligence and dissipating all that is only appearance in the first place, thus getting at the essence, svarupa. Overlays, sublations, conditionings, and false superimpositions are thus done away with by that very mind complex that initially raised them to begin with. The Tantra Philosophy calls this a game of masks that the soul plays, and therefore agrees with the Vedanta and its way of explaining via the five sheaths.

The meditative spiritual art of *Layachintayadhyana* begins with the physical level of things. On its early list of concerns to be dissolved are *bhutas* – objects, bodies, worlds, and gross dualities. The latter of these fatal four, the destruction of dualities, initiates the second stage of *antahkarana-layachintayadhyan* – everything that has to do with the mind and its powers of projection. Ironically, this selfsame mind holds within it the power of dissolution, but most beings are not aware of it. Creation, and the ability to create, is popular with embodied souls, obviously, but dissolution is not. Therefore the soul rarely develops that side of the mind, and leaves it lying fallow.

The Unimaginable Speed of the Mind

In meditation, the advantage is gained by watching the

mind as it engages in all such processes. The trick, for the apt meditator, is to slow the mind down so that the witness can see how it is fashioning the worlds of name and form in time and space. This facilitates two major realizations. First, the soul will come to know that neither god nor devil is creating or destroying the worlds, but rather one's own mental projections, and that this projectionism has participants ranging from The Trinity on down to the ancestors. Among other facets, this realization helps the deluded soul to hoist the Formless Reality, Brahman, back into its position of utter transcendence. Secondly, knowledge of the mind's amazing power of projectionism ushers in the ability for the soul to man the on/off switch of such diverse creationism so as to attain to Peace, *"The Peace that passeth all understanding."* Thus, whenever we see a calm, peaceful, and balanced being, we are actually looking at one who has staved off the desire for mental projection and taken up his or her final residence in the "Abode of Peace." As Swami Aseshanandaji Maharaj once said, *"If you want peace you get God; if you want power you get Rolls Royces."* Thus he warned about charlatans and their penchant for materialism, in the guise of spirituality.

In Tantra, the speed of the mind is called *manojavittvam*. It is one of seven relative stations to gain mastery over, called "The Seven Victories of Involution." The five elements, nature itself, the senses (perception without the aid of the senses), the mind, the mind's powers, and the primal principle — all of these are systematically seen and mastered in due course and time. It all ends in *Sattva Purusha Nytakhyati* — the final conclusion that Matter and Spirit are different in nature. This is why Jesus stated that one cannot seek God and Mammon simultaneously, since they each lead in opposite directions — one outward into the physical universe, the other inward toward the Kingdoms of Heaven.

Faster than the speed of sound is the speed of light, but faster than the speed of light is the speed of thought. To actually see the mind's inner workings is grounds for total amazement. Again, this amazement takes souls in two contrary directions —

one towards the occult powers, and the other towards transcendence. Coming into knowledge of the mental mechanism causes some souls to want to engage all the more in projectionism, what has been termed by the seers as "mass collective mental dreaming." It is only the wise soul who thinks along a different trajectory and begins to experiment with the powers of dissolution. Lord Buddha was one such soul, sitting under the Bodhi tree for weeks in order to both perceive the cycles of *samsara*, and to transcend them as well.

The actual dynamics of mental projection involves an ongoing and unceasing positing of series upon series of thought forms. These happen so swiftly that the owner of the mind itself cannot know what it is actually doing. To slow down or stop a film so as to be able to view each frame individually provides an apt analogy for viewing the mind's workings, stage by stage. This is part of the reason why the seers of India have been examining and recommending that spiritual seekers inspect their deep sleep state in meditation, for that condition, called sushupti, reveals the mind in an actionless mode, devoid of both thoughts and ego — at least temporarily.

A further teaching on this subject reveals that waking and dreaming *(jagrat* and *svapna)* both have cause and effect in them, but deep sleep has only cause; all effect is gone. By understanding this via meditation, the observer can inspect the original cause of form, and of individual self (ego/ahamkara), and thereby gain deep insight and abiding peace of mind.

To complete explanation of the chart on page 35, *bhutalayachintayadhyan*, and *antahkarana-layachintayadhyan* have both been explained. The word, *antahkarana*, in Sanskrit, refers to the "fourfold mind." It consists of dual mind *(manas)*, its thoughts *(chitta)*, its intellect (Buddhi), and its ego element *(ahamkara)*. It is very helpful to know the constituents of one's own mind. It is more helpful to know it with respect to "karana," which reveals that it is the cause of creation, i.e., projection. In the cosmic projection, as well as the collective and individual projection, all manner of blessings and curses exist, side by side.

As we have already seen, the seers thus call projectionism, sankalpa, highly questionable and ultimately undesirable.

The last item of the layachintaya meditation is called *Omkara-layachintayadhyana*. Since "In the beginning was The Word," and the uncompromising meditator wants to arrive at and view the cause of all phenomena, he/she must accomplish the dissolution of all previous stations into AUM, The Word. For AUM is the "Remote Cause" of everything, far beyond, interior, and anterior to the mere physical cause, the theory of the "Big Bang."

Christ meditated well on The Word, and saw it as the origin of all things create. He also stated that it was both "with God" and it "was God." Unfortunately, the twelve apostles did not have Jesus' powers of introspection, and so did not comprehend its greater implications. Instead, they posited it as the origin of all things create, but failed to clarify that the All-Mighty Father was Originless *(ajati)*. Thus, the Christian religion got based mainly on Genesis instead of on Nonduality, as in *"I and my Father are One,"* and *"Be thee as thy Father in Heaven is – Perfect."*

In India, AUM, The Word, is a doorway that opens in two directions – outward into the realms of form, and inward into the Realm of Formlessness. *Omkara-layachintayadhyana* places the final touch on formless meditation, ushering in the "touchless" yoga, called *Asparsha Yoga* by the nondualists. Its irrepressible dissolving power outstrips even the mind's ability in that arena, which is instanced by the fact that mind itself dissolves there, and quite blissfully as well. This state is called *samadhi*. More will be stated about it in forthcoming chapters.

It can now be said that all of the aforementioned forms of meditation in this chapter reflect gradated levels of subtlety, which the *Dissolution of the Mindstream* technique wants to dissolve in successive order. The reader is asked to look back to our original chart on page 3 to plug them all in, as far as each applies. In the meanwhile we will take up a more in-depth study of *Omkara*, The Word, and its importance in every philosophy of India to date.

Chapter Four

Emanation and Dissolution in Vedic Cosmology

A thorough and in-depth study of the chart on the facing page will leave no doubt as to how the Rishis of India, past and contemporary, viewed the eternal principle of AUM, also called the "Unstruck Sound." This august and intriguing name falls in direct accord with the teaching of the bell as evinced in the quote of Sri Ramakrishna Paramahamsa at the top of the chart. The reader is requested to read the quotes on this chart prior to taking the further teachings to come. In short, the sound a bell makes is inherent in the bell itself before the strike takes place.
This fact brings to the fore the teaching on Unmanifested Prakriti as mentioned earlier in this book, which is a major tenet in the Sankhya philosophy of India, one of its earliest. Prakriti, the insentient material energy, is manifest as the physical universe, but the major percentage of it remains unmanifested as the potential for everything to come forth from it over very long periods of time *(yugas)*.

Both manifestation and nonmanifestation are cycles that recur constantly, fashioning all into a cosmic circle, or wheel, that rolls on inexorably. It was the vision of this circle, called the *kalachakra* – the wheel of time ushering in birth and death – that caused Lord Buddha to sit for weeks under the Bodhi tree to find a way off of it. The way to freedom was thereby mapped out by Him once again in the age in which He lived (550 BC).

In this vein, we assign the dual function of the bell two words by which its inner secret is revealed for examination, those being emanation and dissolution – the latter word being closely associated with the title of this book.

Omkara — The Great Cause
Emanation and Dissolution in Vedic Cosmology

"It has been revealed to me that there exists an Ocean of Consciousness that is without limit. From It comes all things of the relative plane. Therefore I give the illustration of the bell's sound, 'T-o-m.' The strike of the bell is like the falling of a great weight into the ocean; waves rise on all sides. Spiritually speaking, the relative rises from the Absolute; the causal, subtle, and gross worlds and bodies appear out of the Great Cause; the waking, dreaming, and deep sleep phases rise out of Turiya. And just as millions of brahmandas rise in the Ocean of Chidakasha, they merge in It again. The Lila merges into the Nitya." Sri Ramakrishna

"In the Beginning was the Word, and the Word was with God, and the Word was God."

"Gates of the body closed, the mind confined in the heart, fixing the life-force in the head, engaged in yoga, uttering Om, Brahman, and thinking of Me, that one who departs the body attains to the Supreme Goal." Krishna

"Pranava is the lower Brahman, and it is the higher Atman. Having known Pranava one attains to Brahman." Gaudapada

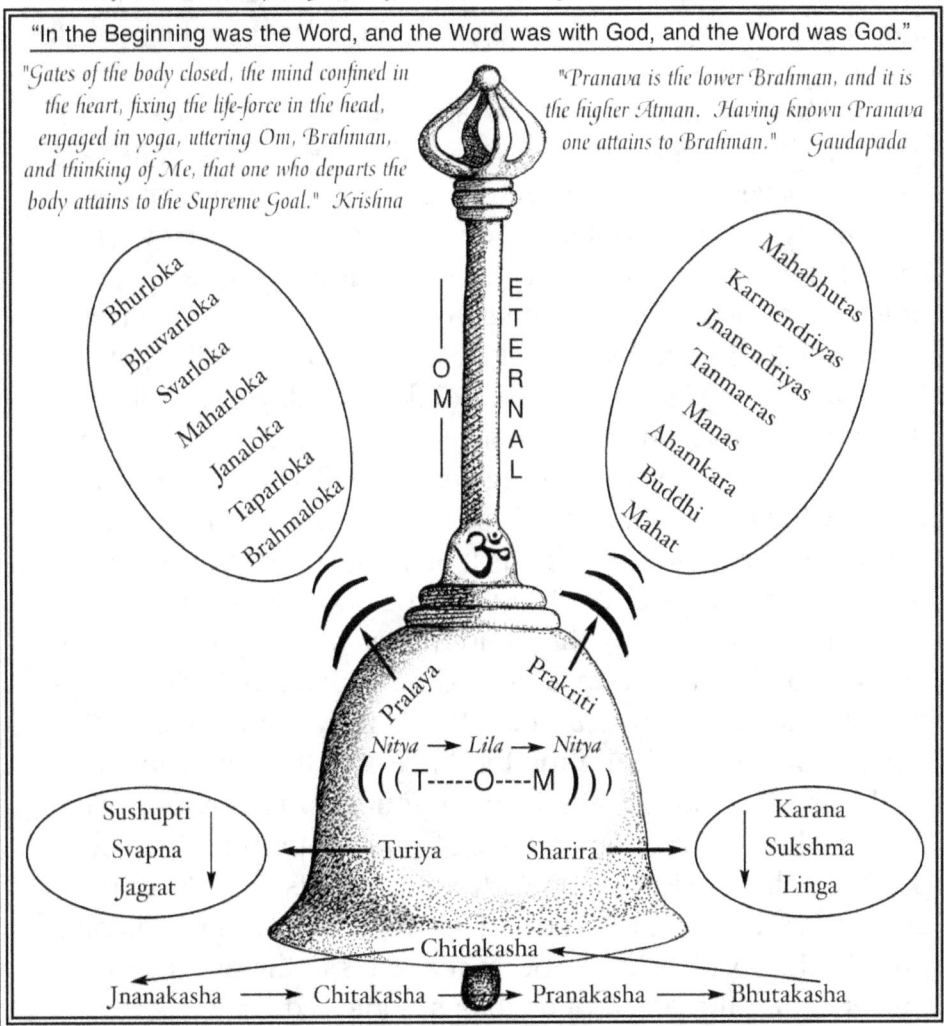

"All universes in space and time lie within Om. With knowledge of the Word, and how cosmic projection goes forth, one can follow the shining rays of Jnana-wisdom straight to the Source, penetrating all brahmandas. Then the Mother of the Word will immerse one in the Ocean of Consciousness." Svayambhuva Manu

Chart by Babaji Bob Kindler   Property of SRV Associations

Sacred Triputis

One edifying way of approaching the Unstruck Sound, its profound meaning, and this chart (page 49), is to take up Christ's cryptic saying which appears on the chart. Those words must have stultified John and the other disciples, which is probably why Jesus wanted them to spend more time meditating in the garden of Gethsemane. For they would have to take on the "press" of the weight of the world after his passing, and He knew that to do so without knowledge of The Word would be well nigh impossible.

Most all great teachings are composed of three parts; most all great problems are composed of two. These latter are called dualities; the former are called *triputis* in Indian philosophy. Every problem contains a doorway out of its narrow environ. For instance, the duality of virtue and vice offers up the option of transcendence. One is a gold chain, and the other is an iron one. The preference of no chains opens up the path to freedom. In similar fashion, that difficult duality called life and death has for its solution Eternal Life. In this way is the way out of bondage kept clear for struggling souls. The reader is invited to study the chart on the facing page (page 51) for more edification on the art of sacred triputis in Indian philosophy. Essential quintuplications are also introduced there for reflection.

Moving back to the chart under study (page 49), the teaching of Christ to John, then, has three parts to it. The first is that *"In the beginning was the Word"*; the second is that *"the Word was with God"*; and the third is that *"The Word was God."* As the chart demonstrates, the bell's sound and its various overtones all have their origin in the bell, and are present there even prior to it being struck. Similarly, all thoughts, worlds, objects, and bodies, have their origin in The Word, and exist in potential prior to the solidification process that ends in the production of matter. Thus, the origin of all things is inferred.

In the case of the second part of this triputi, *"....the Word was with God"* indicates that everything not only emanates from the Word, but that it returns there as well. Here, a case can be

Vedic Triputis and Quintuplications

"This divine expression is definitely declared to be the Supreme Brahman in manifested form. In that is the Triad. It is the firm support, and it is the imperishable. Knowing the inner essence of this along with its sets of triputis and quintuplication processes, the knowers of the Vedas become devoted to Brahman, merge themselves in It, and are released from birth and death." — Svetashvataropanisad

"The Three Prerequisites for Atmajnan, knowledge of your Soul, consist of the destruction of illusory thoughts, the gaining of quiescence of mind, and the ability to merge in Brahman at will. Lauded among the supreme knowers as Atma-tripti, they will stand you in good stead, no matter what the impediments thrown up by the mind in maya. By these three, and other divine triputis, may you attain to the Atmic state, free of all stains and pains." — Lord Vasishtha

made for the fact that when the vibrations of the bell emanate forth, they simply dissipate in the ethers after fragmenting into various levels of distortion. This may be true of the physical vibration, but the subtle vibrations trace their source to the power of the bell to strike, peal forth, and ring. This is where the materialists fail to comprehend great teachers and teachings, preferring to rely only upon what the senses can provide by way of outer verification. But as the Mundakopanisad states, *"The five senses are defective by nature, since they are verily outward moving only."* Physical ether, *"Bhutakasha,"* contains only the external worlds – planets in outer space. The *"Kingdom of Heaven within"* consists of multiple realms and countless worlds on subtler levels of existence. Four other *akashas*, subtle spaces, rest there. These are eternal portions of what is *"....with God."*

Vibrating Spheres of Consciousness

In brief, all manifestation returns to The Word in the same way that the essence of the bell's vibration returns to the bell itself – to be sent forth again at the time of the next cosmic sounding. This teaching is explained in many ways on the chart on page 49. On the upper left side are seen the seven lokas, from *Bhurloka* on through to *Brahmaloka*, Bhurloka being the realm of earth and its surrounding planetary systems – all essentially consisting of the five elements alone in various permutations. These worlds will end in *Pralaya*, dissolution, after extremely long periods of time in cycles.

On the upper right-hand side of the chart, the vast extent of emanation is explained in yet another way. The cosmic principles, *Tattvas*, ranging from the five elements *(mahabhutas)* to the ten senses (in two sets of fives) to the subtle elements, the mind, ego, intellect, and finally the Cosmic Mind, are all seen flowing out of the Primal Word. The vibration emanating from the Cosmic Mind, vested in it by the Unstruck Sound of AUM, permeates creation at all levels – gross, subtle, and causal. All these are seen to get dissolved back into *Prakriti* – specifically "Unmanifested" Prakriti, after successive *Yugas*.

Emanation and Dissolution in Vedic Cosmology 53

On the lower left-hand side of the chart under study we find a unique way in which some Rishis explained the process, simplifying it without making it any less profound, to be sure. The triputi of *Jagrat, Svapna,* and *Sushupti* — waking, dreaming, and deep sleep, has its unalienable correlation with the Primal Word as well. The Word has three *Matras,* or particles: A, U, and M. The first designates the waking state of man's consciousness. The "U" stands for his dreaming state. The "M" symbolizes his deep sleep state. Since name and form are fashioned, maintained, and dissolved, under the auspice of these three states, all accompanied by the presence of vibration, or the lack thereof, the seers thereby point out the profound significance of The Word.

And across the chart, on the lower right-hand side, are the three bodies — *stula, sukshma,* and *karana.* These correspond to the states of waking, dreaming, and deep sleep, being the apparatus that the soul uses to shift levels of consciousness, all within its own boundless territories. *Stula* is the gross body, made of the five elements and other material substances — flesh, fat, bone, etc. The *sukshma sharira* is the mental body (also called *linga*), or subtle body. Its contents are more of thought, conceptualization, the power of projection, etc., as we have been studying so deeply thus far. Finally there is the *karana sharira,* which is the unseen, usually undetected, causal body. Mating it up with the deep sleep state is one of the only effective ways of drawing attention to it, and of studying it, what to speak of even knowing of its hidden existence.

Of course, meditation is the best way to encounter the subtle body, particularly meditation of the formless variety. Since all the worlds consist of vibration at various levels of intensity and degree, it would stand to reason that when the rapt meditator succeeds in quelling the thought vibrations of the mind, he will experience a type of emptiness that is not that of the void, nor that of the listless vacancy of the mind, but rather one of peace and subtle bliss. In deep sleep this process and its result takes place via loss of consciousness, but in meditation the idea is to keep one's awareness present and watchful in order to see what transpires and witness it when all falls silent.

The penultimate teaching key on the chart under study (page 49) is at the bottom, referring us back to an earlier mention of the Five *Akashas*, or subtle ethers. In order to give a clearer picture of what is meant by the mind's inner regions, or what exists at the level of subtle and causal vibration of The Word – what Jesus referred to as the *Kingdoms of Heaven within* – a chart outlining The Five Akashas (facing page) is now introduced.

Playing with Dolls

Using the familiar analogy of the five Russians dolls, indicating how each akasha lies within the next – from gross into subtle into causal, ending up in Causeless Reality – a grander view can be gained of not only how these realms interconnect and impinge upon one another, but also of all that lies within them. This teaching provides excellent answers to questions about where our loved ones go after leaving the body, where the ancestors abide in the interim *"bardo"* before their next incarnation into the physical world, and the presence of the subtle locations that the gods and goddesses preside from – as well as where enlightened beings hold their causal bodies in order to be of help to embodied beings in lower vibratory spheres.

Taking the smallest doll first, we see that it symbolizes the *Bhutakasha*, or physical worlds. Much like the causal and subtle realms, and Formless Reality Itself, the physical universe is also infinite. Countless stars and planets spread across the vast and boundless expanse of material space.

The provisional essence of these is elemental, however, consisting of earth, water, fire, air, and ether, these five also falling from gross to subtle in their respective appearance and manifestation. Since in Vedic Religion and Philosophy, *"All is Brahman,"* and *"Only Reality Is,"* the Indian Rishis refer to this realm as *Saguna Brahman* – Consciousness sporting with attributes. It resembles children playing with dolls, the only problem

The Five Akashas of Vedanta Philosophy

"Like five Russian dolls of diminishing size, which neatly nest inside of one another, all ending up as one all-inclusive unit, similarly do the five atmospheres through which name and form manifest all reside within each other — from causeless to causal to subtle to gross — each holding multiple dimensions, countless worlds, and myriad beings." — Babaji Bob Kindler

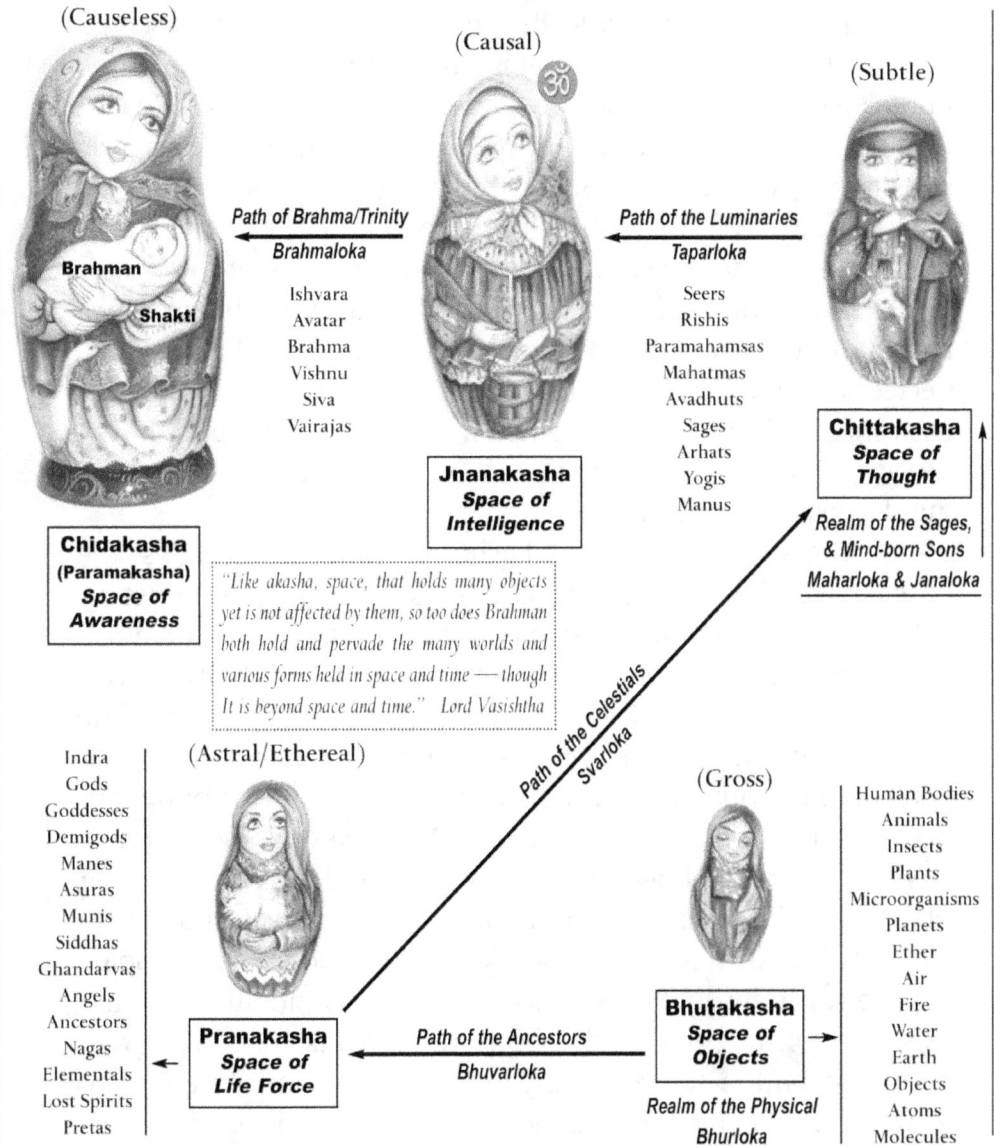

(Causeless)

Brahman / Shakti

Chidakasha (Paramakasha)
Space of Awareness

Indra
Gods
Goddesses
Demigods
Manes
Asuras
Munis
Siddhas
Ghandarvas
Angels
Ancestors
Nagas
Elementals
Lost Spirits
Pretas

(Causal)

← Path of Brahma/Trinity
Brahmaloka

Ishvara
Avatar
Brahma
Vishnu
Siva
Vairajas

Jnanakasha
Space of Intelligence

"Like akasha, space, that holds many objects yet is not affected by them, so too does Brahman both hold and pervade the many worlds and various forms held in space and time — though It is beyond space and time." — Lord Vasishtha

(Astral/Ethereal)

Pranakasha
Space of Life Force

← Path of the Ancestors
Bhuvarloka

(Subtle)

← Path of the Luminaries
Taparloka

Seers
Rishis
Paramahamsas
Mahatmas
Avadhuts
Sages
Arhats
Yogis
Manus

Chittakasha
Space of Thought

Realm of the Sages,
& Mind-born Sons
Maharloka & Janaloka

Path of the Celestials
Svarloka

(Gross)

Bhutakasha
Space of Objects

Realm of the Physical
Bhurloka

Human Bodies
Animals
Insects
Plants
Microorganisms
Planets
Ether
Air
Fire
Water
Earth
Objects
Atoms
Molecules

"All forms, multifarious in manifestation and expression, being aspects of the wisdom-word, like drops of rain falling into torrential rivers, enter that massive Ocean of Consciousness called Brahman. Each akasha, from gross to subtle — physical, pranic, mental, intellectual, causal — will dissolve into the Paramakasha, that supreme space of pure, conscious Awareness." — Lord Vasishtha

Chart by Babaji Bob Kindler   Property of SRV Associations

with said sport being the pain and suffering that naturally accompanies it, and a whole host of miseries that are inherent in it if the mind that fashioned it does not, as the mother exhorts them to do, "play nicely."

In the sidebar next to the smallest Russian doll is seen a copious list of some of the beings and principles that infill the Bhutakasha. All of these are parts and fragments of Reality, whether insentient or not. That is, human bodies are naturally insentient, but the one Soul occupying them is profoundly Sentient; otherwise higher intelligence would not be there in the human mind and absent in all the other denizens of this realm. The presence of intelligence is a sure giveaway to the existence and underlying presence of Atman/Brahman. And the interconnectedness of all beings and all things is also a signal of the pervasiveness of Brahman, though at first, and along the way towards effective dissolution, it poses certain obstacles for the mind seeking nonduality.

Intersecting the Bhutakasha on subtler levels is the *Pranakasha*, the space of vital energy. Certainly, some substantial traces of prana can be seen in the physical world in the form of energy in food, electric energy, kinetic energy, and the power of animation in bodies and the five senses. It is just that the source of this power remains unseen and unknown to the major percentage of humanity. That is why Jesus wanted to bring it to our attention, and did so by stating, *"Man does not live by bread alone."* He could have meant that mankind needs nature, or objects, or pleasures, or occupations — wives, fishes, and loaves, etc. — but that does not sound like His teachings. Some opine that He was referring to the Spirit by this profound utterance, but as we are finding out, God is both free of cause and effect, and unable to be the cause for anything in the realm of name and form. It is ever pure and perfect, free of all modifications.

As was clarified earlier, the knowers of Truth declare that the cause for everything is The Word when it was *"in the beginning"* and *"was with God."* Divine Reality has no beginnings. It is Eternal. It cannot be the cause of anything, but is ever pristine

Emanation and Dissolution in Vedic Cosmology 57

and perfect, beyond even the very ideas of origin and inception.

In the Pranakasha, the space of vital energy, prana is king, and all moves by its presence and flow. In fact, when the yogis attempt to control the mind and its thoughts and tendencies in order to gain transcendence and freedom, they know they must first get ahold of the prana and control it. Prana carries all things, all beings, to their respective realms *(lokas/akashas)*, and this is the case of all that has to do with the mind as well, like its thoughts. Prana carries beings from waking, to dreaming, to deep sleep as well, and back again.

Souls leave the physical body via the prana, which travels along unseen nerves called *nadis* that connect it to wherever it is headed in its play, its sport, its dream life. As we can see by the list in the sidebar of the chart on page 55, there are a host of beings that are inhabiting the Pranakasha who do not live by bread alone. They would be very displeased if the moderns dwelling in the Bhutakasha forgot to pay them homage, or suddenly opted for a materialistic position alone and decided that they did not exist! Plagues, famines, and pestilences might be visited on such uncaring, insensitive creatures, could they not?

Perhaps this is the reason why all the great sayings of the seers from India, reflected in the many scriptures, are initiated and ended by the refrain, Peace, Peace, Peace — *Shanti, Shanti, Shantih.* The illumined souls want to be sure that all beings maintain the spirit of worship. The first exclamation of Peace is for the beings in the physical world, the Bhutakasha. The second repetition of Peace is for the beings in the life heavens, basically the Pranakasha and Chittakasha. The last intoning of Peace is for all beings "On High," in the causal regions — may they shower their grace upon us, eternally.

The Chittakasha is the space of mind per se. The Sanskrit word, *"chit,"* signifies thought; also the "stuff of the mind," meaning every mental occupation that the mind takes up, a host of them listed in the chart on page 31. The only difference between the Chittakasha and the realm it dissolves into, called the *Jnanakasha,* is the degree to which intelligence has been realized.

The beings that inhabit the Chittakasha are called siddhas, sages, and the more attained munis, while the more refined beings peopling the Jnanakasha are seers, yogis, rishis, and the like. Great minds do abide in the Chittakasha, for certain, just like genius' mix with ordinary beings on earth, but a higher level of realization attends upon those frequenting the Jnanakasha. This is where illumined souls return after leaving the physical realm, at least and as long as they have work and service to render to suffering beings. As an addendum to this teaching, the reader can examine the chart on the facing page to see how Buddhism looks at the soul's transmigration, particularly those who have overcome root ignorance and awakened to their true nature.

As can be seen, there are some Ten Pure Inner Lands that the Bodhisattvas reach for and attain. All of these correspond roughly with the *Chittakasha, Jnanakasha,* and *Chidakasha* of the chart and system presently under study on page 55. Briefly, each land within is attended by certain fruits of attainment, and also by often strict and stiff qualifications for their attainment. On all levels of Consciousness, these are based upon the aspiring and masterful soul's burgeoning ability to assist other souls in their spiritual journey towards Enlightenment.

It is most revealing to notice that all darshanas, not just Buddhism, are important of attainment to the Buddhist practitioner, and that the knowledge of all of them contribute substantially to gaining unconditional liberation, as well as to the mature spiritual adeptship that excels in teaching others to do so as well. This system contains everything important to one's crucial experience of Divine Reality, whether it is called Buddha Nature, Prajna Param, Atman, or Brahman. Far beyond taming base passions and extirpating root evils, the eschelons of spirituality itself are proclaimed and revealed in such a fine system.

Returning to finish our play so we can carefully put away our dolls, the final akasha, called *Chidakasha,* is both the approach to formlessness, and formlessness itself. All of the previous Russian dolls are now neatly tucked inside of it, which illustrates the final consummation of the *Dissolution of the*

Dasabhumikas — The Ten Pure Lands
or Ten Stages of Bodhisattvahood

1) Pramudita-bhumi (Land of Joy)
* Full spiritual awakening takes place   * Bodhisattva vow is taken
* Vow of dana, generosity, is accepted   * Wishes for karmic merit are renounced
* Egotistic pursuits and all dharmas are perceived to be empty

2) Vimala-bhumi (Land of Purity)
* Shila, spiritual discipline, is perfected
* Practice of dhyana & samadhi are intensified
* Lapses in concentration are removed

3) Prabhakari-bhumi (Land of Radiance)
* Attains the 4 Stages of Absorption
* Attains the 4 Stages of Formlessness
* Acquires 5 of the 6 Supernatural Powers

4) Archismati-bhumi (Blazing Land)
* Burns away all false conceptions
* Begins to develop nondual wisdom
* Achieves right exertion
* Works on the 37 Limbs of Enlightenment

5) Sudurjaya-bhumi (Hard to conquer Land)
* Meditates to realize The 4 Noble Truths
* Works on the 37 Limbs   * Destroys all doubts

6) Abhimukhi-bhumi (Wisdom-view Land)
* Gains insight into conditioned arising
* Transcends need for discriminating thought
* Achieves shunyata — perception of voidness
* Perfects wisdom — Prajna

7) Durangama-bhumi (Far-reaching Land)
* Attains skill means to guide others
* Can be reborn in any form of choice
* Transcends all possibility of regression

8) Achala-bhumi (Immovable Land)
* Gains freedom from obstacles
* Knows time of personal Buddhahood
* Transmits own merits to others

9) Sadhumati-bhumi (Pure Mind Land)
* Attains full bodhisattvahood   * Has all 6 Abhijnas
* Has the 8 Liberations   * Has all 10 Dasabalas
* Has the 4 Certitudes   * Knows all dharmas & transmits them

10) Dharmamegha-bhumi (Land of Dharma-clouds)
* Has wisdom, compassion & boundless virtue
* Confirmed Buddhahood   * Has mature Trikaya   *Abides in the Buddha fields

---

Dhyana
(The 4 Stages of Absorption)
1) Akushala, Vichara, Vitarka, relinquishing desires via conceptualization and discursive thought.
2) Thought dissolves to promote inner calm and one-pointedness.
3) Equanimity (upeksha), alertness, awareness, and well-being
4) Eternal awakeness, abidance

Arupasamadhi
(The 4 Stages of Formlessness)
1) Stage of limitless space
2) Stage of boundless awareness
3) Stage of nothingness
4) Stage beyond aware & unaware

Abhijnas — 6 Supernatural Powers
1) Wealth and power 2) Divine hearing
3) Perceiving other's thoughts
4) Recollection of past lives
5) Divine sight
6) Extinction of impurities & certainty of enlightenment

Dasabalas — 10 Powers of a Buddha
Knowledge:
concerning deaths and rebirths
concerning purity and impurity
concerning the ripening of deeds
concerning absorptions, liberations
concerning the paths leading to worlds
concerning the abilities of other beings
concerning the constituents of the world
concerning exhaustion of defilements
concerning tendencies of other beings
concerning the possible & impossible

Chart by Babaji Bob Kindler
Property of SRV Associations

Mindstream technique perfectly. All that is left over in this realmless realm are those blissful traces of conscious causal form called Trinity, *Avatar*, and *Ishvara*. Even the overseers of the five akashas and seven worlds are in the process of dissolving here. The Prana, too, has gone into hiding now, dissolving into the *Mahashakti* whose mighty, puissant power it belongs to. As Lord Vasishtha has stated, *"All beings and all things are always busy merging into Reality, like multiple raindrops falling into torrential rivers."* All has returned to its formless Essence, proving once again the timeless words of the Indian Rishis — that *"All is soluble into Brahman."*

Chapter Five

Seven Levels of Cause and Effect

Departing a bit from the traditional way of describing levels of cause and effect in Vedanta, yet drawing out the hidden inferences that the tradition nevertheless holds and strives to relate, the following chapter dedicates itself to a many-tiered edifice symbolically reminiscent of a magnificent castle with numerous floors and multiple chambers. The luminaries thought in similar terms when they perceived this cosmic structure, stretching back within human consciousness to the fathomless depths that even the intellectually informed mind has little idea of.

"*My Father's Mansion has many chambers*" was the way that one illumined soul, the Christ, described this internal vision. About it, Lord Buddha, fresh from many days of deep meditation, stated, *"Architect of this universe of name and form, I have seen thee. Now I will not build homes in relativity any more, not homes of wood or stone, not homes of flesh and bone, and not homes of wise conception."*

It should be noted, then, that a vision of the Cosmos that includes all levels of existence is not necessarily a totally positive one. Besides, there is the Formless Realm, not to be discounted, and it is That which the greatest of all beings espy and aspire for in deepest meditation. Its appearance puts to shame even the marvelous beauty of the projected realms, and It is free of all the problems and obstructions associated with them as well.

The Vedantists call these impediments by the title of the *Six Transformations*, while the Buddhists list them as the *Six Billows*. In numbered order, they are: birth, growth, disease, old age, decay, and death. Other considerations include hunger and thirst. It is the presence of unsatisfiable, inescapable principles such as these that cause the discriminating seeker of Truth and Transcendence to take a deep, hard look at the Cosmos, on all its many levels. By the word "cosmos" here, is not meant only the physical universe with all its many planets in space, but also the many-tiered, multi-layered *"Mansion"* of Consciousness that lies within. To inspect this more closely, a chart has been created and placed on the facing page.

Starting at the bottom of the chart and working our way up, the first level of cause and effect is called the *Material Cause.* It is based on food. This strata of consciousness is dense, where vibration has congealed, where thought has become materialized and solidified into objects. It is also desire prone, necessity prone, and survival prone. As was mentioned before, if embodied beings are able to perceive the presence of prana in their food, and in objects, and comprehend the subtle meaning and overall import of vital force, both philosophically and spiritually speaking, the Material Cause will offer up many keys and profound secrets towards higher understanding.

As it is, however, the senses of mankind, combining with the objects of the senses, create an attraction that leads to attachment to matter, and finally to the belief that matter is all that exists – and in the end, to that tenebrous and purblind idea that even the human being is a product of matter. Unfortunately, living beings seek no further than this world for any deeper answers to their problems, problems that surface as a result of attachment to the physical world and what it has to offer. Even intelligent beings – doctors, scientists, law-givers – get swept up in limited beliefs that are founded in and based upon bodily existence alone. Studying the Material Cause and its list on the facing page will reveal this dilemma.

The Distinction between Mind and Brain

Food, its energy, sperm, ovum, and the physical body, all have a primal connection. When the fetus matures and is released from the mother's womb, it begins growing, still on the energy from food, and the ten senses continue to develop. The

▶▶ CAUSALITY, ORIGINS & REINCARNATION ◀◀

"The ability to project worlds of name and form, seemingly actual, in space and time, furthers the circle of influence of cause and effect. With the curbing of the unruly mind's penchant for mayic manufacturing comes instant freedom from the trammels of relativity. This liberating process is facilitated by tracing origins." King Janaka

Causeless Cause

Brahman ⇅ Shakti
ॐ

Remote Cause

Ishvara
AUM
Mahaprakrti
Mahat

- Primordial Soul
- Unstruck Sound/Word
- Unmanifest Nature
- Cosmic Mind

"Inner analysis brings the first real glimmerings of spirituality. In that light the soul perceives the assumed happenstance of cause and effect. In a series of deep recollections it scrutinizes life, even to infanthood, and glimpses past lifetimes. By perceiving its origin it courts freedom." Vasishtha

"Differentiation between jiva and Ishvara is right if one is a dualist. But for Advaitans this notion of jiva as distinct from God is the cause of bondage." Swami Vivekananda

Cosmic Cause

Maya
Vidya
Kala, Desha, Nimitta
Niyati, Kalas, Raga
Purusha

Evolution

- Form & Formlessness
- Higher Cognizance
- Time, Space, Causation
- Cosmic Laws, Phases, Attraction
- Individual Soul

"The moment that cause and effect comes to an end one realizes God. That is one's last birth. This, plus the practice of spiritual discipline and time, are the main factors in the attainment of spiritual knowledge." Sri Sarada Devi

Subtle Cause

Buddhi
Ahamkara
Chitta
Manas
Kama
Karma

- Intelligence
- Projected Self/Ego
- Thought
- Mind
- Desire for Life
- Desire for Activity

"Souls embody to enact an array of karmas which place them under the influence of the unforgiving laws of cause and effect. Not all of these lifetimes, these dream-streams of conditioned awareness, are founded in negativity. Many there are, masters of mental projection, who wrap themselves in the fabric of maya to merely enjoy ephemeral pleasure." Queen Chudala

Chart by Babaji Bob Kindler
Property of SRV Associations

Primordial Cause

Pancha Tanmatras
Prana - Pancha Vayus

- 5 Subtle Elements → Audibility, Tangibility, Visibility, Flavor, Odor
- 5 Life Forces → Prana, Apana, Vyana, Udana, Samana
  (Inhalation, Exhalation, Digestion, Aspiration, Circulation)

Efficient Cause

Prakrti & 3 Gunas
Pancha Mahabhutas

- Nature/Gunas → Tamas, Rajas, Sattva (inertia, activity, balance)
- 5 Elements → Earth, Water, Fire, Air, Ether

Material Cause

(Chart by Babaji Bob Kindler   Property of SRV Associations)

Antahkarana
Pancha Jnanendriyas
Pancha Karmendriyas
Deha
Maharaja
Sukra
Mukhyaprana
Annam

Involution

- Human Brain
- 5 Cognitive Senses → Hearing, Seeing, Touching, Tasting, Smelling
- 5 Active Senses → Speaking, Moving, Handling, Procreating, Excreting
- Physical Body
- Ovum
- Sperm
- Vital Energy
- Food

"If higher knowledge is not already in the soul, then rebirth continues and there will be no other recourse than to suffer cause and effect. Even striving for light will not bestow any real benefit, for to seek enlightenment without the mantra, the teachings, and the guru, is like trying to grow crops only at night." Vasishtha

human brain is as yet undeveloped as well. Everything about the physical condition bespeaks of dependence on time and circumstances. As this process displays itself in front of humanity as a whole, the entire mass becomes mistakenly convinced of the actuality of transformation. This could be called a natural conclusion, but what is unnatural is the shortsightedness that accepts transformation as an ultimate end. Decay is one of the Six Transformations. From food to the human brain, all is subject to it.

It is therefore that the truly wise person uses the brain to discover the mind. Though connected, these are two different mechanisms. Not content to accept the finality of death at the end of life after so much development has been undergone, and so many victories won, the enterprising soul perceives the distinction between the human brain, an organ that decays, and the human mind, an eternal principle of ultimately Cosmic proportions that is imbued with major powers that the brain can neither hold nor comprehend — causal memory, conceptionalization, intelligence, wisdom, foresight, revelation, and more.

Successive Echelons of Effect

The mind is subtle; it is the *Sukshma Sharira*, the "subtle body" of man. The brain is just a fleshy organ, rather like the heart and lungs. As we can see by the chart's outlay (page 63), entering into the realm of the mind is tantamount to gaining direct proof of and access to all the causes for existence, from the Remote Cause on down. Thus, the mind *IS* the Kingdom of Heaven within; where else would it be? Out in the physical ether?

To discover the real Source of manifestation, then, the intrepid spiritual traveler must find a way to pierce through the many veils covering Its revelation — familial, social, hereditary, political, religious, scientific. Anything of a conventional nature, along with all mistaken concepts that foist upon the seeking soul a host of untenable and unacceptable fallacies, must be discriminated carefully and put down, quelled. Some of these are: a mere materialist perspective; a one-lifetime only scenario; a "the world-is-my-oyster" type of thinking; the worship of my ancestors alone predicament; a seven-day creation theory ending in eternal damnation; the narrow and hypocritical view that there is only one incarnation of God and all must accept it and no other; the backwards idea that all other religions but my own are foreign and inferior. This list culminates in present times with the short-sighted declaration that "the world of objects is made of material particles, and that's the final word on everything" conclusion. As Jesus said about all such things devilish in nature, "Get thee behind me."

The next level of cause and effect is what we are calling here the *Efficient Cause*. Nature and its hidden modes are that. The five elements stand behind all that is in food, and are themselves infused by the five pranas. A deeper understanding of this connection can be had by looking back on the main chart on page 3. The elements, the ten senses, the five tanmatras, and the five forms of prana are connected, and form a web of density whose strands are unlikely to be snapped by anyone but the sedulous soul that is unremitting in its resolve for Enlightenment.

Importantly, the three gunas are a part of this subtle net of appearances, and will persist into the realm of the Cosmic Cause as well. They will first be discovered by the soul at this level of cause and effect called the Efficient Cause. It can then begin to perceive their role in everything from nature, to action, to moods, to mind. Inertia, dynamism, and balance infuse everything, and the key to getting beyond these is that attainment of peace, bliss, and equanimity via conquering these three gunas.

The chart presently under study on page 63 next displays the *Primordial Cause*. Prana is that. To discover the secret that opens the door beyond the physical universe, and to unlock the powers needed to pierce through all of the conventional ways and beliefs listed above, is to perceive the prana, court it, gain control over it, and utilize it to gain mastery. What is it that one must master? The mind. Far beyond the limited powers of the brain, the mind is responsible for the appearance of name and form in time and space based upon cause and effect.

This may be hard to accept at the outset, but teachings are given to clarify that the individual mind is not alone in this projection process. The collective mind and the cosmic mind are all considered as "Mind" in toto by the luminaries. The reader is asked to look at the chart on page 63 and find the *Mahat* under the Remote Cause heading, *Manas* under the Subtle Cause heading, and the *Antahkarana* under the Material Cause heading. These represent the individual, collective, and cosmic mind as a composite whole, with the power to *"fashion and level mountains."* The powers of nature, the gunas, and the prana are all found in the mind.

And if we look at the next echelon of cause and effect we shall see why. Intelligence, the assumed self, thought, mind, the desire for life, and the desire for activity, are all classed under this heading, called the *Subtle Cause.* When one considers it, that represents a mass of power and an abundance of forces. It is no wonder that Sri Ramakrishna said about the human being in possession of such a mental complex, *"What a lot of mischief is caused by this small being measuring only a few cubits tall."*

To put it in condensed form, the mind has for its legions the five elements, the five senses of action, the five senses of knowledge, and the five pranas. Its powers are sankalpa and vikalpa. Its counselors are the ego, the intellect, and the myriad of thoughts that pass through it daily, all at lightning speed.

Pushing on, or in, it becomes clearer how the mind can manage all these powers and forces, for it is intrinsically connected with the *Cosmic Cause.* Here lay principles, most of which are unknown to the masses, and even to beings who have managed to enter the subtle regions of the mind and begin to utilize its talents and abilities. Most important is the *Purusha* itself, the real Soul of mankind, far outstripping the ego mechanism who poses as the real Self until Purusha is realized. Just as the mind has all the aforementioned legions and counselors, the Purusha is endowed with its hosts of principles — knowledge of cosmic laws, higher intelligence, and perception of God with form and beyond form. The chart presently under study (page 63) lists all these in both Sanskrit and English for the reader's edification.

Also important of further mention is the fact that the Cosmic Cause is responsible for containing the subtlest forms of concepts like time, space, and causality – *Desha, Kala,* and *Nimitta.* Phases of time too long to comprehend *(kalas)* are also stored there, as is the often stultifying principle called *Raga,* the power of attraction. Naive persons may cite a number of different theories about what holds everything together, from God and mankind, lover and beloved, mother and child, right on down to the adhesion of atoms and molecules. The simplest answer, however, is love. But as can be seen, maya is still present at this level, and where maya persists, love is often only a caricature of itself. Only Divine Love earns the right to call itself by that august name.

Such Love, pure and unconditional, is verily possessed and showered upon beings by Mahaprakriti Herself, also called Mahashakti. At the level called the *Remote Cause* is where the intrepid spiritual luminary is now beginning to locate this real Source of Existence. The Primal Shakti, Her Trinity (Mahat), Her select sons and daughters (Ishvara/Ishvari), and The Word, all exist and coalesce at this most prime and pristine zenith of Conscious Awareness.

Importantly, the soul that is ushered into this land of pure radiance sees the end to cause and effect, as cited in the quote from Sri Sarada Devi, the Holy Mother, placed in the sidebar adjacent to the Cosmic Cause. The reader is invited to read all the pertinent quotes from various luminaries associated with every echelon of cause and effect listed on the chart.

Only the *Causeless Cause* is left to inspect. What can be said about it except that *"Brahman cannot be the cause of anything,"* as stated earlier, and in the scriptures. Where Brahman and Shakti are one, like fire and its heat, like water its wetness, there lies the purest of the Pure. No issue comes forth from It, yet it is the Ultimate Foundation, the Underlying Substratum, for all that burgeons forth from The Word at the behest of the Mahashakti. So sayeth the Tradition.

This chart and its teachings (page 63) is based upon the sacred art of *Utpatti* — tracing origins. Not surprisingly, this inward trajectory facilitates the *Dissolution of the Mindstream*. Like placing articles of clothing into a chest of drawers after they have been washed and ironed neatly, just so, the Mother of the Universe guides the ascending soul in accounting for all the principles of relative existence, from gross to subtle to causal — or, from material, to efficient, to primordial, to subtle, to cosmic, and furthest inward to the most remote of all — so that it can effectively put them away in order to see its own Sentient Self that is beyond all projection and all manifestation.

This blessed arrival is called Enlightenment, Self-Realization, Illumination, and by a host of other sweet names, the aspiring embodied soul makes an adamant sojourn away from the realms of dream projection in ignorance of its Self (Atman), and towards the Essence of Awareness that is the very nature of Existence, Knowledge, and Bliss Absolute — *Satchidananda*.

To close this chapter, a chart that is both indicative of this inward journey, and associated with all the levels of cause and effect just put forth on our chart, is placed on the facing page for examination. May living beings come to see life as a purposeful excursion inward to The Source, instead of a swiftly passing span of several decades spent in vain surface pleasures and ending in death. As the great Swami Vivekananda used to put it in his letters to his western students: *"The only so-called higher beings are departed, and these are nothing but men who have taken on another body. This is finer, it is true, but still a man body, with hands and feet and so on. And they live on this earth in another akasha, without being absolutely invisible. They also think and have consciousness, and everything else like us. So they are also men, and so are the devas, and the angels. But man alone becomes God, and they all have to become men again in order to become God. You are God, I am God, and man is God. It is this God manifested through humanity who is doing everything in this world. Is there a different God sitting high up somewhere?"*

Phases of the Soul in Relativity

"The jiva at first remains in a state of ignorance. It is not conscious of God, but of matter and multiplicity. It only notices the many things around it. Upon attaining knowledge it becomes conscious that God dwells in all beings. But on attaining higher wisdom it discards both knowledge and ignorance and talks of nothing but God day and night." ≈ Sri Ramakrishna Paramahamsa

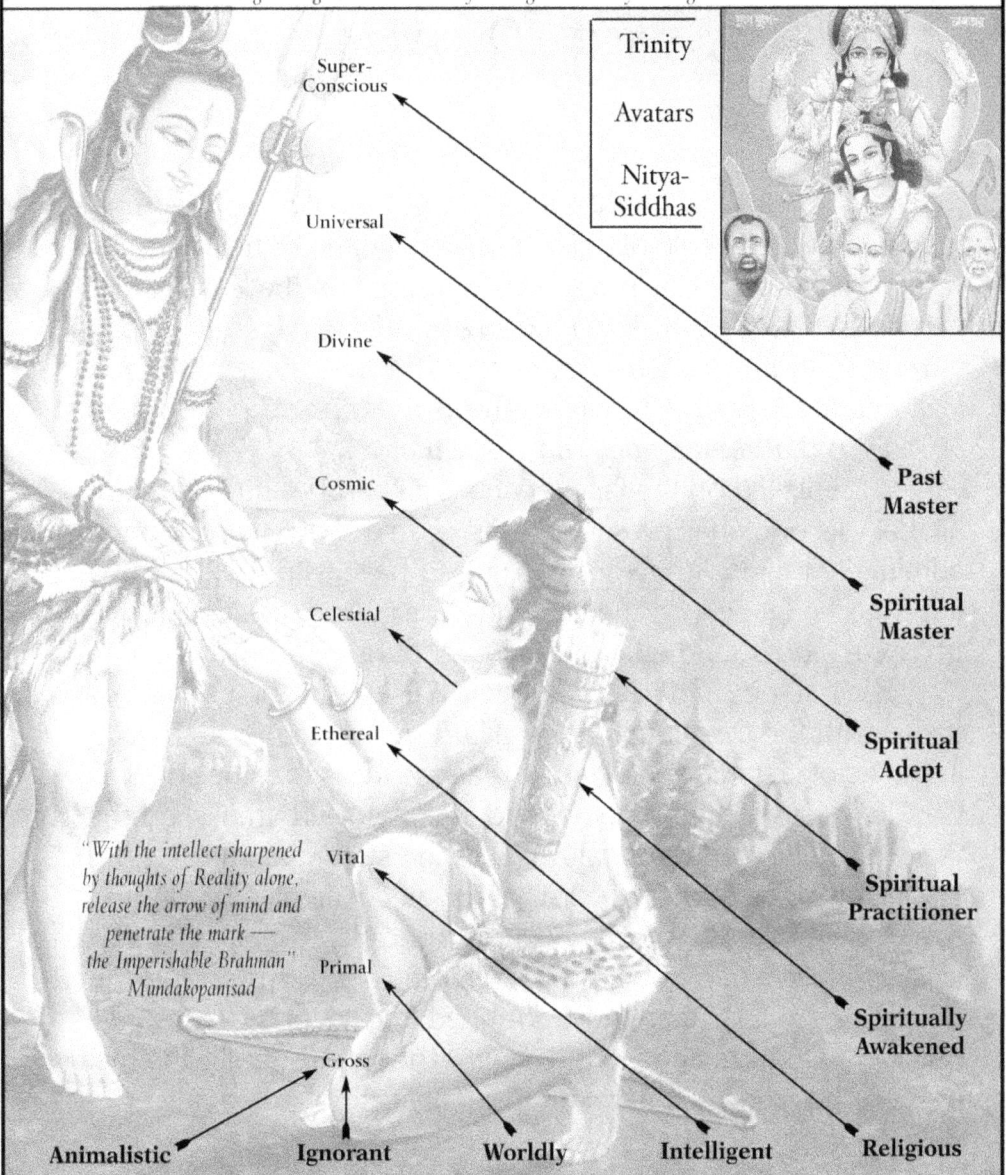

Trinity

Avatars

Nitya-Siddhas

Super-Conscious

Universal

Divine

Cosmic

Celestial

Ethereal

Vital

Primal

Gross

Past Master

Spiritual Master

Spiritual Adept

Spiritual Practitioner

Spiritually Awakened

Religious

Intelligent

Worldly

Ignorant

Animalistic

"With the intellect sharpened by thoughts of Reality alone, release the arrow of mind and penetrate the mark — the Imperishable Brahman" Mundakopanisad

"There is a greater accumulation of God in man than in other creatures. God is born as man for the purpose of sporting as man. He is thus called Narayana. Rama, Krishna, and Chaitanya are examples of this. By meditating on the Divine Incarnation of God one meditates on God Itself. If God can manifest through the image, then why not through man?" ≈ Sri Ramakrishna Paramahamsa

Chart by Babaji Bob Kindler   Property of SRV Associations

Chapter Six

A Simple Overview

It was Swami Vivekananda's way to make abstruse philosophy and subtle spirituality comprehendible to humanity, all without watering it down or compromising it in the least. Once, he wrote: *"I have clear light now, free of all hocus-pocus. I want to give Truth dry hard reason, softened in the sweetest syrup of love, and made spicy with intense work, and cooked in the kitchen of Yoga so that even a baby can easily digest it."*

Displayed on the facing page is a chart designed to place all that this book has presented thus far in a simple light, though admittedly the aspiring soul is going to have to put forth some effort and engage in some study in order to put away all forms of *"hocus-pocus"* and attain to the goal of human existence.

What the chart here has to teach us is, of course, in accordance with the *Dissolution of the Mindstream* technique. Taking in the whole chart at one glance, the essence is that the soul will want to destroy the obscene, renounce the seen, transcend the unseen — all in order to realize his divine stature as the Seer.

Taking note of all the lists associated with all four of these strata, the reader will see many of the principles — individual, collective, and cosmic — that have been introduced previously in other systems. They are now arranged in categories that everyone can recognize and identify with — though ironically, the real purpose has mostly to do with disidentification.

The Seer, His Constitution, and Its Implications

The station of the Seer is the most impressive of all that is shown here. That is, the obscene is evil; the seen is alluring; the unseen is perplexing; but the Seer is admirable, reverential,

The Seer, The Seen, The Unseen, & The Obscene

"I transcend what is seen and what is unseen. I am the Supreme Seer. This multitude of beings manifest themselves and go to the unmanifest state continually, and thereby subject themselves to rebirth in good and evil wombs. They do not know of the Eternal Existence which never changes, never perishes. But those who perceive It by knowing the unity of the Seer, the Seen, and the Unseen are never born in the gross worlds again."   Sri Krishna

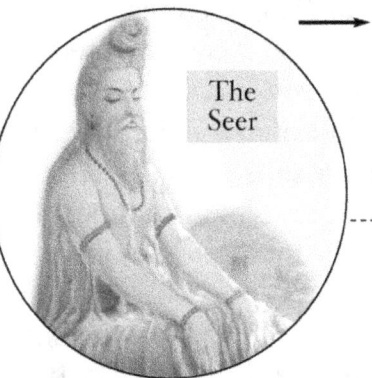

The Seer →
Brahman   Atman   Chaitanya   Chetana
Parabrahma   Mahavishnu   Paramasiva   Mahamaya
Videhamukta   Jivanmukta   Maharishi   Sakshi
Samadhi   Nirvana   Moksha   Mukti   Turiya

The Seen

Ether/Space   Air/Wind   Fire   Water   Earth
Electricity   Motion   Rotation   Gravitation
Humans   Animals   Insects   Micro-organisms
Oceans   Forests   Rivers   Plants   Flowers

→ Ishvara   Devas   Celestials   Ancestors   Disembodied
Om   Cosmic Mind   Cosmic Laws   Subtle Elements
Intelligence   Thoughts   Mind   Ego   Prana   Gunas
Atomic Particles   Quarks   Neutrons   Sub-atomic

The Unseen

Violence   War   Domination   Genocide   Rebirth
Selfishness   Hatred   Deceit   Insincerity
Ignorance   Egotism   Delusion   Vanity   Weakness
Worldliness   Body-Attachment   Superficiality

The Obscene

Chart by Babaji Bob Kindler   Property of SRV Associations

and to be worshiped and followed as an exemplar. The host of names, hardly exhaustive of the many possible Sanskrit references, proclaim the seer to be that rare type of soul who has transcended maya, put away the gunas, and neutralized all personal karmas to attain the ultimate station, "Enlightenment."

Given the uniqueness and sparsity of such a soul in relativity, a deeper look will familiarize the student with some of the attainments that the luminary hosts and wears so naturally, so effortlessly. Coming back to the chart under study later, the chart on the facing page (page 73) reveals the inner constitution of such an uncommon being, showing him or her up to be one of exceptional character and unrivaled realization.

First, and as indicated by the fine sloka from the *Nirvana Upanisad*, we see that the main attainment of any luminary is the destruction of the sense of "I-ness." In any list of principles to be penetrated and transcended, the ego certainly qualifies as one of the subtlest to perceive, and one of the most difficult to be rid of. In fact, Sri Ramakrishna has proclaimed that it is impossible to dispel it completely so long as one remains in the body. For that reason it is to be minimized so that it will not intrude on and spoil the soul's bid for higher realization.

All of the items associated with the seer's existence while he is in the body are listed on the chart on the facing page, and it can be seen by studying them just how differently the seer treats them as compared to most of humanity. For instance, most beings would have as their ideal the attainment of wealth, family, name and fame, objects, and pleasure, etc., but the authentic seer only thinks of Ultimate Reality and his sempiternal abidance there. And who is the preceptor of most living beings? With regard to spirituality, they have none. But the seer, seeing his precarious predicament in the embodied state, cast amidst the vagaries and vicissitudes of maya, wastes no time in seeking out a wise guru and taking refuge there.

Looking over the host of considerations on this chart, the seer seeks protection only from the presiding deity that resides in his very own heart, called the *Antaryami* – "the Inner ruler

The Integral Constitution of the Luminaries

"Those qualified souls who are fit to study the Upanisads are protectors of the field in which I-ness is destroyed. To them, all beings and the world are just pure Consciousness. To them, talk about the uprooting of karmas amounts to mere words, for the illusion of I-ness has been cremated and spread about in the cemetery of Self, of Brahman. For others, these luminaries represent a ship with which to cross the ocean of earthly existence." — Nirvana Upanisad

Chart by Babaji Bob Kindler
Property of SRV Associations

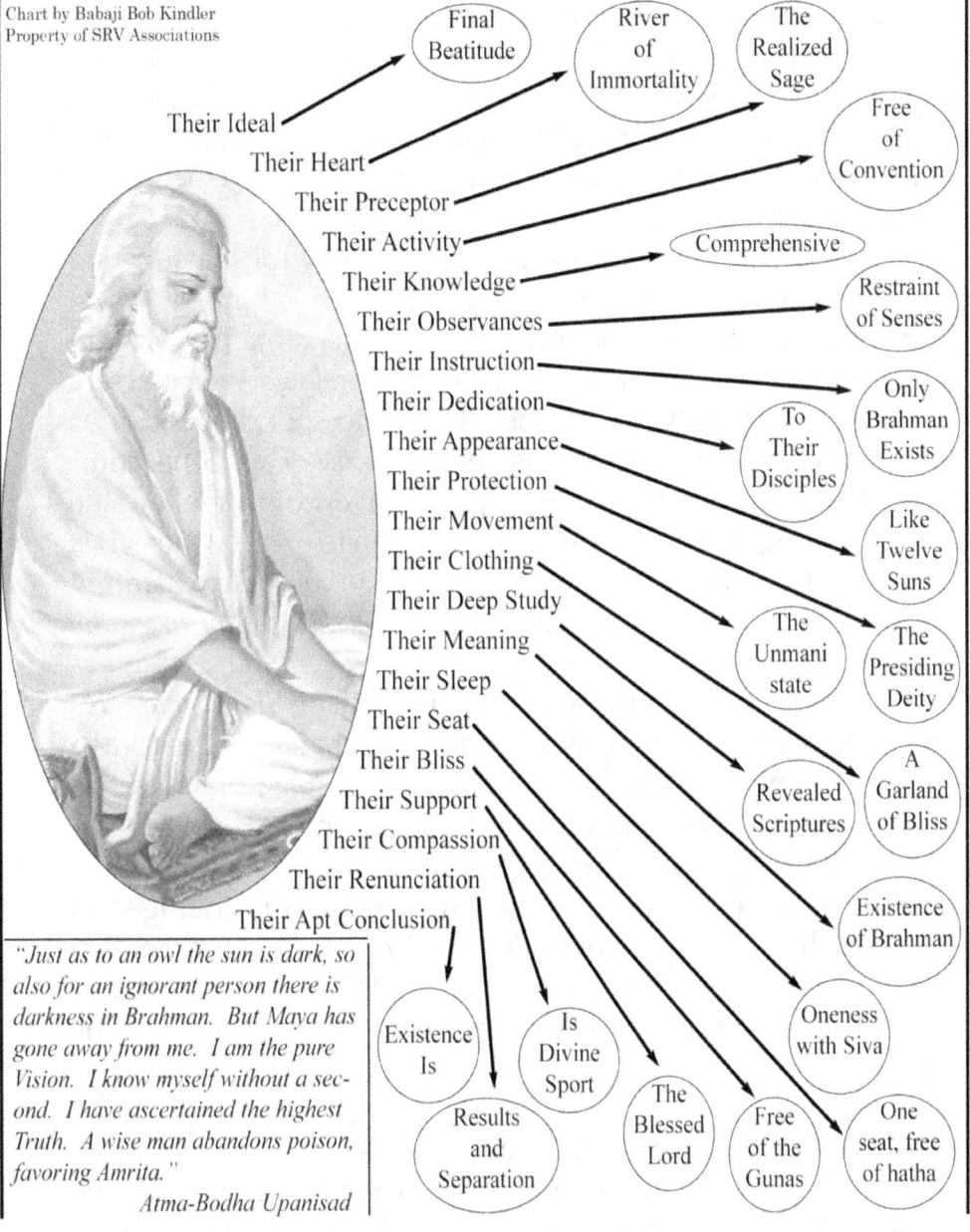

"Just as to an owl the sun is dark, so also for an ignorant person there is darkness in Brahman. But Maya has gone away from me. I am the pure Vision. I know myself without a second. I have ascertained the highest Truth. A wise man abandons poison, favoring Amrita."
— Atma-Bodha Upanisad

Their Ideal — Final Beatitude
Their Heart — River of Immortality
Their Preceptor — The Realized Sage
Their Activity — Free of Convention
Their Knowledge — Comprehensive
Their Observances — Restraint of Senses
Their Instruction — To Their Disciples
Their Dedication — Only Brahman Exists
Their Appearance — Like Twelve Suns
Their Protection — The Unmani state
Their Movement — The Presiding Deity
Their Clothing
Their Deep Study — Revealed Scriptures
Their Meaning — A Garland of Bliss
Their Sleep
Their Seat
Their Bliss — Existence of Brahman
Their Support
Their Compassion — Existence Is
Their Renunciation — Is Divine Sport
Their Apt Conclusion — Results and Separation
— The Blessed Lord
— Free of the Gunas
— Oneness with Siva
— One seat, free of hatha

Immortal seated in the Heart." Others take their security in all the ephemeral things of the world that change constantly and cannot be relied upon. Regarding that all-important study that souls must make while sojourning in the worlds of name and form, the few who do study subjects with any interest other than pleasure, fasten upon lower knowledge in tandem with the physical universe, and even that mainly for making money. But the seer scours and scrutinizes the revealed scriptures to find keys to the secrets of the inner realms. He strives to find and utilize a way out of maya, a way beyond nature and its aforementioned transformations such as disease, decay, and death.

And is the seer thus lacking in empathy for the suffering of others, looking only for a clear way out for himself? Even given that most beings are not looking to separate from nature and its painful transformations, the chart relates that the seer enters the body only to demonstrate how to sport in the worlds of name and form, in the *"Fields of the Lord."* This IS his compassion, for only by shining example will a few others follow, the majority being too bound into desire for finite objects and cycles of karma to even want to get free. As the *Atma-Bodha Upanisad* puts it: *"A wise man abandons poison, favoring Amrita – the Nectar of Immortality."*

The consummate seer concludes that *"All Existence Is."* His renunciation, accomplished long since, has settled into two modes of mature detachment: one from results, or fruits; the other, from identification with any form or semblance of separation whatsoever. Oneness, or "not-twoness," is his firm stance. Nothing can alter it; he is stable. The reader is encouraged to look on the chart at the other forms of nonconventionality that attend upon the seer and his unique life. His very existence is an example of what is possible in terms of true Freedom for the embodied soul.

The Seen, Its Meaning, and the Keys It Offers Up

Returning to the chart on page 71, we next encounter "the Seen." Though several of the items in this category cannot necessarily be seen by the naked eye, nonetheless they are present, and help form the building blocks of the physical universe. As far as the *Dissolution of the Mindstream* technique is concerned, this makes them fairly simple to espy and transcend.

The Father of Yoga, Patanjali, has labeled them with the interesting and suggestive Sanskrit word, *"alambanas,"* indicating that they ought to be used as stations for meditation. Taking water, for instance (or any of the five elements), the meditator will focus on it to see all that is in it, and all that is inferred by it. After such intense scrutiny is implemented, everything that involves or concerns water is "seen" by the "seer" — purity, flow, inundation, saturation, liquidity, expansiveness, even matters like swimming, diving, drowning, etc. Following on the trail of water, then, the meditator is led to and finds out about many matters heretofore unseen and hidden, such as his fears, his personality, his potential abilities, and his past lifetimes, to name a few. Such is the advantage that meditation has over western science and psychology, adding multiple dimensions for deep consideration, all indicative of gaining deeper and higher wisdom.

The Unseen, Its Subtlety, and Its Inscrutable Nature

Undoubtedly, the "Unseen" category is necessarily set up for more advanced levels of encountering and dissolving. Most of these have to do with the realm of the mind as a territory, and not a mere mechanism for holding thoughts. Particles of matter appearing at different rates of vibration have been added to this category, more to suggest a doorway into subtler regions than to create a good fit, categorically. When particles become so miniscule and fine, their rate of vibration impossible to accurately measure, it is time to look beyond the physical universe to find where the energy that causes them to vibrate comes from and goes to. It is not just that matter and energy are convertible; this is intriguing only on the physical level. It is far more interesting that matter has a source of origin in prana, mind, intelligence, and other inward principles.

The old conundrum about whether deities, i.e., gods and

goddesses, celestials, etc., exist, where they abide, whether they are real, and so forth, gets satisfied in this comprehensive and composite view of things. Everything that can be imagined exists, but if one's criterion for existence is founded upon sensual perception only, on the physical level only, then literally everything else becomes a mere phantasm of the mind. Ironically, the luminaries peg matter and objects as the actual phantasm, and insights coming from our recent Quantum Physics has verified this — though unbeknownst to those who presently champion it.

Celestials, gods (devas), ancestors, the disembodied — all of these and more inhabit the unseen realms, invisible because one needs subtle senses to view them. These are precisely what one acquires and refines in early meditation, so it is no surprise to spiritual preceptors that students practicing the art of meditation suddenly have internal commerce with their "deceased" ancestors, along with visions of gods and goddesses, darshan with illumined beings, and more.

Cosmic laws are also on the list of the Unseen on the chart under study (page 71). The reader will also notice that the subtle elements are present too, inferring that there are subtle senses (as just mentioned above) to detect and utilize them. The easiest way to understand this at the outset of practice is to think of how many worlds, relationships, beings, and objects, the mind creates (projects) in one's dream state every night, and also how they are "destroyed" upon waking.

Sri Ramakrishna utilized this reference symbolically by citing the fine metaphor of the young boy who delights in building sand castles on the beach before high tide comes in, and gets equal satisfaction by watching them destroyed before his very eyes by the power of the ocean's surging waves. It is through meditation, mainly, that the five subtle senses and five subtle elements — exactly like those ten encountered in the waking state — are perceived and put to work. One can see how important the soul's facility around them will be when it comes time to implement the *Dissolution of the Mindstream*. The castles one builds, whether of earth, energy, or mental concept, must come apart sometime. The yogi is one who wants to do it ahead of time, long before the approach of death, for instance.

The Insanity of Obscenity

The final category on the chart under study, humorously called the Obscene, though really no laughing matter, offers up its own sets of teachings as well. They are important to heed, because the obscene level of human existence is usually the first level of things that must face dissolution. In other systems this is referred to simply by pointing to the need for the destruction of ignorance. For, unbeknownst to most beings, these evils have their cause, thus their solutions, in the mind. For instance, a dictator may think about war for some time, brooding on its possibility, and that mental energy that he places into the subject is bound to have its effect. War then ensues. Thought is father to the deed. This teaching not only makes sensitive beings more careful of their thoughts, but also shows how everything has its origin in the mind.

The following chapter, and its chart, will focus a bit upon this root ignorance in the mind — the producer of the "Obscene" — particularly in accord with how to overcome and transcend it in Vedantic fashion.

Chapter Seven

The Unreal Never Is, The Real Never Ceases to Be....

A fogbank, though it causes all manner of deception, trepidation, and the fear that proceeds from both, is nevertheless devoid of substance. Such is the case with ignorance as well, as described by the Indian seers. Ignorance is also the main cause of suffering in more than one of India's great philosophical darshanas. Called *avidya*, this ignorance originates from the primal depths of the mind, its root, so it is also called *mulavidya*. In Yoga, avidya is the first of five *kleshas*, impediments to union with God, and in Vedanta it is called the first of five hells the soul deludedly subjects itself to. For more clarity, the reader can refer back to the Curtain of Nescience chart on page 19.

A knowledgable person, a worldly-wise being, an intellectual giant – there is a lack of awareness, a missing essence, in all of these. It is the embodied soul's cluelessness that its true-nature is Divine, is one with Reality. That he is unawares reveals the presence of mulavidya. Mankind is not an animal, not a body, not nature, nor is he even a mere mental complex – though the latter is a firm indicator of his superiority over all other creatures.

Who Am I?

In short, man is the Soul, the Essence of Consciousness Eternal who has taken on layers of form, probably for many different reasons. These reasons can even be gradated, high to low: he wants to express his formless awareness; he wants to manifest higher wisdom on earth; he wants to teach spiritual wisdom to all beings in all realms; he wants to sport in form; he desires to help suffering beings caught in the web of their own deception, i.e., avidya; he has become unsure and wants to prove his birthless and deathless condition; he has forgotten that he is immortal, and therefore has to be reborn in order to remember it again; he has lived several lifetimes in ignorance and is therefore under the press of karmas that drag him back into the body against his will. Finally, and lowest, he is completely lost and has fallen onto the wheel of birth and death in total ignorance of his true nature. There are other reasons for his incarnation too, and admixtures of all of the above operating as well.

The entire list of reasons to incarnate can be placed under two crucial perspectives, those being whether or not man is conscious of his true nature — in other words, free of ignorance on that score. If he lacks this singular bit of knowledge which is the basis for all higher wisdom, and the lynchpin for unraveling maya and getting to the Truth Itself, then all the book-learning in the world will avail him not. As Swami Vivekananda has put it: *"Where seekest thou? That freedom friend, this world nor that can give. In books and temples vain thy search...."* As Jesus put it: *"What will it avail a man to gain a kingdom but lose his soul?"* As Shankara put it: *"Adore the Lord! Adore the Lord! Adore the Lord, you fool. When the time of your body's death approaches, what good will your worldly knowledge do you?"*

Without knowledge of his divine nature, then, all the worlds of name and form in time and space become a series of bad dreams for him, and even basic peace of mind remains far away — what to speak of the fact that all of nature exists in him, and that all its manifestations have sprung from his own mind.

The essential spiritual question, *"Who am I?,"* then, is simple. I am Existence, Knowledge, Bliss Absolute. And what is Enlightenment? It is constant remembrance of the fact that *"All is Brahman — time, space, living beings, and the world,"* as the nondual scripture, *Vivekachudamani*, states it. When asked once if a man should be reborn, Swami Vivekananda answered plainly: *"I certainly hope he will not, not until he can do so in full Consciousness."* This statement of his proves that man's nature is, as he himself was wont to say, potentially divine, and that bringing that divinity into the embodied condition can and must be done. Vivekananda's own life, of course, lived in full view of contemporary world society, proves it further.

Empty of Ignorance

The chart on the facing page is introduced so that the student and practitioner can both know about the inscrutable presence of ignorance, as well as the dynamics of internal sadhana that will disperse it. After all, this is the main purpose of the *Dissolution of the Mindstream*, for when ignorance disappears, the Soul will come to the fore of its own volition, naturally. As the Upanisads express it: *"The Atman, the Indivisible Self in all beings, all things, is realized by knowledge, moderation, austerity, and veracity, all of these constantly cultivated. When mental impurities dissolve due to this practice, the seer beholds it naturally, existing everywhere – even here in this very body."*

The journey up and out of ignorance can be explained by using the two trajectories shown on the pyramid on the chart on page 81. The left-hand side evinces the path towards fulfillment via love and peace/equanimity, while the right-hand side shows the path to transcendence utilizing study and self-effort. The base of the pyramid shows underlying root ignorance into which most beings are born.

The path to fulfillment is basically initiated by rising beyond fun and excitement to happiness, and leaving that limited station behind for joy. All of these have rajas in them, or frenetic energy, and can be used for the soul's ascension. Of course, yearning and sincerity must be present in the soul, for both paths, in order for headway to proceed.

Contentment, the fifth level of the first path, is what is aimed for, and the aspirant will get it by the gaining of wisdom via experience. Abiding for a time in contentment will bring about Peace, which is its own reward. But there is hardly a higher attainment than equanimity, or *upekshanam*, for it remains unruffled under all conditions and situations. From it, unalloyed

The Disappearance of Ignorance

"One day I awoke and my ignorance was gone, gone, utterly gone! Who can conceal the Truth? Who can keep a blazing fire tied in a cotton cloth?" — Ramprasad Sen

Fulfillment | Discipline

Bliss — *Ananda* | **Transcendence** — *Para*

Equanimity — *Samatva* | **Attainment** — *Sampadyate*

Peace — *Shanti* | **Self-Effort** — *Sadhana*

Contentment — *Tripti* | **Austerity** — *Tapas*

Wisdom — *Jnana* | **Contemplation** — *Manana*

Joy — *Mudita* | **Scriptural Study** — *Svadhyaya*

Happiness — *Sukha* | **Holy Company** — *Satsangha*

Excitement | **Dharma**

———— **Ignorance / Avidya** ————

"If a man but tastes the bliss of God, he runs after it thereafter. It matters little to him then whether the world remains or disappears." — Sri Ramakrishna

"At the time of creation, people had wisdom from their very birth. Consequently, they at once realized the unreal nature of the world. They renounced it and practiced austerity. They were liberated in no time." — Sri Sarada Devi

"We believe that every being is divine, is God. Every soul is a sun covered over with clouds of ignorance; the difference between soul and soul is only due to the difference in density of these layers of clouds." — Vivekananda

"The secret of religion lies not in theories but in practice. This is all I have to preach. Doctrines have been expounded enough. There are books by the millions. Oh, for an ounce of practice!" — Vivekananda

"Perhaps one practices japa and austerity in this life. In the next life one intensifies the spiritual mood and in the following advances it further, and thus spiritual evolution goes on." — Sri Sarada Devi

"The happiness of the worldly man slowly declines as his spiritual joy becomes deeper." — Sri Ramakrishna

"The nondual scriptures point the way to Moksha, that most elevated condition that is the very atmosphere of Divine Reality." — Lord Vasishtha

"The happiness of the world is transitory. The less you become attached to the world, the more you enjoy peace of mind." — Sri Sarada Devi

"Whenever I contemplate the teachings of the dharma, I cannot help but share them with others." — Milarepa

"From peace, a fuller, richer, nobler knowledge will dawn, to be tempered further still by the apt instructions proceeding from an illumined preceptor in conjunction with the revealed scriptures. Then, through sententious striving you shall come upon, in a state of spiritual exaltation, that Truth which you are seeking, and which puts to death even the most delicate and diaphanous tendrils of ignorance." — Lord Vasishtha

Chart by Babaji Bob Kindler Property of SRV Associations

and uninterrupted bliss — *Ananda* — will certainly arrive.

The right-hand side of the chart begins with the student seeking the *dharma*, which has already been described as being beyond the level of morals and ethics. These two qualities are expected of the noble soul by the preceptors, as the yamas and niyamas of the eight-limbed tree of Yoga reveal — that is, such attributes as nonviolence, truthfulness, purity, and so forth. But beyond both the iron chain of immorality and the gold chain of morality lies the shackle-freeing stroke called dharma. The aspirant after higher wisdom must lay his hands on that, for it consists of teachings on how to gain the secrets of spiritual life for himself, not just how to be good and virtuous. In other words, he is interested in perceiving his true divine nature, not merely watching the endless exchange of good and bad as they play across the infinite expanse of the human mind.

From dharma, as the chart on page 81 displays, proceeds holy company. This will come on its own when the seeker courts teachings, vows, and basic spiritual precepts. He or she will need a wise teacher for this, and for other reasons. The seeker will also need to inspect the scriptures under the tutelage of such a guru, and follow up this in-depth perusal with deep reflection on the truths contained therein. This contemplation is essential for both the instilling of wisdom into the human mind, and for the resultant dissolution of ignorance that ensues thereafter.

Simply put, the mindstream will have to be attenuated of all its wayward tendencies, and if this process of implementing the first four stages does not entirely wipe them away, then the following and more aggressive move called austerity, or *tapas*, will surely succeed. This is the way of *Sadhana*, a course followed by those who are adamantly seeking the Truth which will not brook any impediments or delays in that search. About this sagacious way, and contrasted to the way of fulfillment, asceticism, sublimation, and even grace, Sri Krishna states in the *Uddhava Gita*: *"It may be, that occasionally, and among very strong souls, a few will reach enlightenment by the power of their own innate will and practice."* One can well imagine, then, how much effort will be required for this feat, and how approving and appreciative the seers are of these rare types of beings.

Sadhana's aim is attainment. Attainment qualifies the now more advanced adept for the experience of samadhi, in all its lower to highest stages. Samadhi is transcendence — not only of the worlds of name and form in time and space based in causality (maya), but also of the ignorance and suffering that veiled this sublime realm of Consciousness from inner view in the first place. Ironically, once the soul has tasted, or retasted, its true essence once again, it feels as if the ignorance that was recently present was never actually so; it cannot even remember what it felt like to "be" ignorant. Thus, as Sri Krishna puts it in the Bhagavad Gita, *"The Unreal never is."*

That *"The Real never ceases to be,"* however, is now much more endearing to the awakened soul. Even more, he now commands a mind that is pure, having successfully dissolved all self-formulated things back into it. Ignorance, the suffering it caused, dangers such as materialism and hypocritical fundamentalism, limitations like worldliness and intellectualism, the ordinary mind and all its facets, cosmic laws and cosmic principles — everything has now been mastered, stripped of fear and doubt, and tucked back into the Primal Word from which it came. He can now enjoy the bliss of fulfillment in Samadhi. The Mindstream will never again sporatically leak and spurt randomly and thoughtlessly. If he so wills, it will only venture forth, in innocent play, to portray the divine sport of pure, conscious Awareness for all beings to see.

The reader is invited to study all the quotes of luminaries that have been collected on the chart on page 81 in accordance with all its steps and stages. The two pathways described there actually intermingle with one another, based upon the temperament of the seeker. It must be added that some forms of ignorance persist into later stages of spiritual evolution. Therefore, a full and complete passageway must be opened up from ordinary mind, to collective mind, to cosmic mind, and beyond. The next chapter will reveal more about this winsome way.

Chapter Eight

Total Dissolution of the Mindstream

Some final teachings and details about the *Dissolution of the Mindstream* practice can be given here in the final chapter. For these purposes, a repeat copy of the original chart, displayed earlier on page 3, is shown again on the facing page. The presence of ignorance is inferred in such a chart, at least for those ones who have fallen out of Yoga and are suffering from forgetfulness and its evolutes. For such as these, the process is to be undergone in meditation so as to free the mind from superstitions, false ideations, and persistant misconceptions that have collected over lifetimes. Further, remembering the inner cosmology of human existence is tantamount to accessing conscious births with awakened parents in auspicious conditions.

For the adept, however, this chart represents a journey the facile soul must make whenever it descends to grosser vibratory spheres. As Sri Aurobindo once put it, *"The awakened soul goes up and down the amber stairs of birth and death at will."* These cosmological cross sections of consciousness become like a familiar neighborhood to such beings, and they remember them from lifetime to lifetime. Taking a body and giving it up, what other beings call birth and death, are simple matters to the luminary, though this cosmic move is not without a price to pay.

A Brief Recap

In this vast and interdependent quintuplication process that is constantly going on, and over immense spans of time that even by itself constitutes sufficient cause for the soul's forgetfulness, the problem of impurities is a considerable one. In this subtle grinding process, a cosmic dust is always rising as a result,

Dissolving the Mind Stream
The Formless Meditation of the Upanisads

"When a sugar cube dissolves into hot liquid, it first breaks in half, then into small chunks, then into granules, and finally there is nothing left but sweet liquid. Similarly, when the mind moves towards authentic meditation, it first contemplates the dual world, then the many teachings, then living particles of its own intelligence, and finally enters full immersion. What remains then is one blissful, indivisible homogenous mass of pure, conscious Awareness." — Babaji Bob Kindler

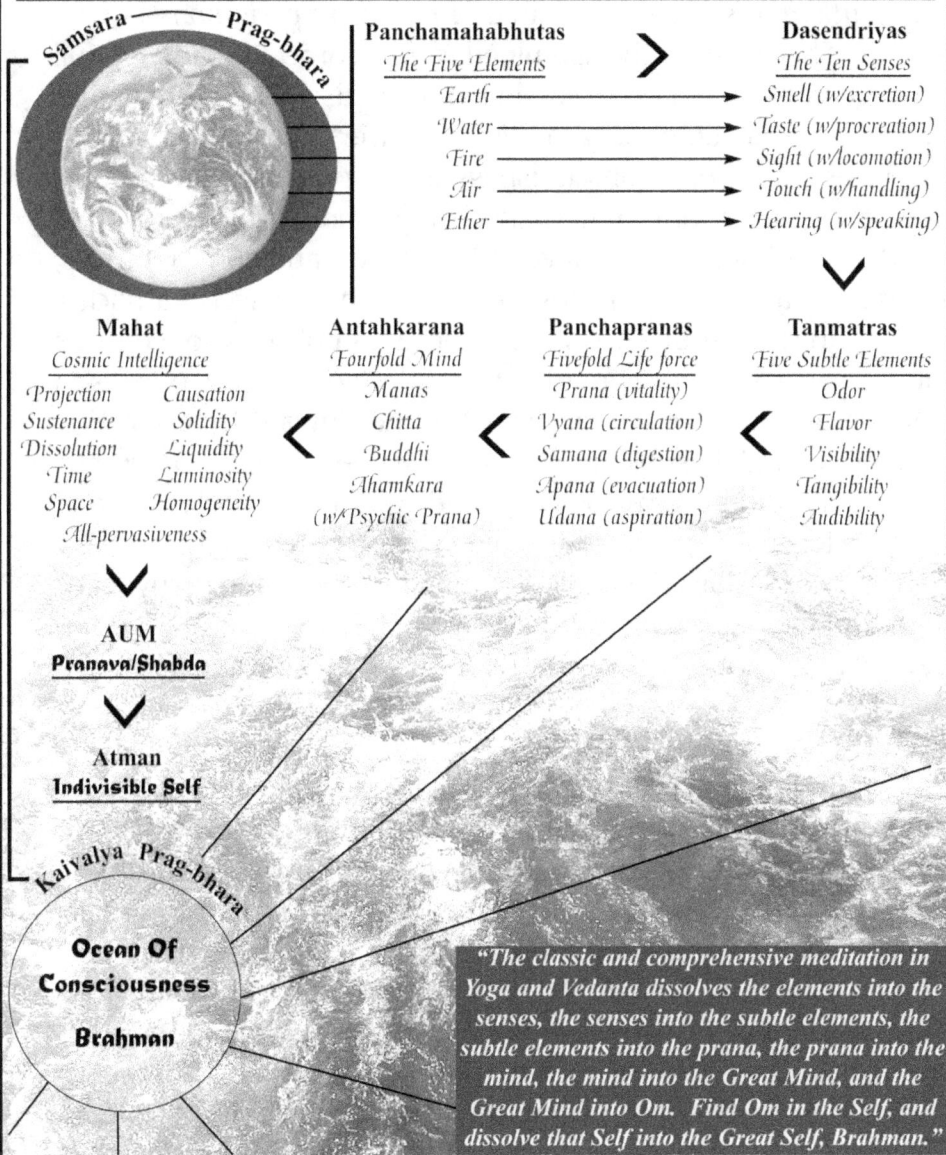

Samsara — Prag-bhara

Panchamahabhutas
The Five Elements
- Earth
- Water
- Fire
- Air
- Ether

Dasendriyas
The Ten Senses
- Smell (w/excretion)
- Taste (w/procreation)
- Sight (w/locomotion)
- Touch (w/handling)
- Hearing (w/speaking)

Mahat
Cosmic Intelligence
Projection   Causation
Sustenance   Solidity
Dissolution Liquidity
Time   Luminosity
Space   Homogeneity
All-pervasiveness

Antahkarana
Fourfold Mind
Manas
Chitta
Buddhi
Ahamkara
(w/Psychic Prana)

Panchapranas
Fivefold Life force
Prana (vitality)
Vyana (circulation)
Samana (digestion)
Apana (evacuation)
Udana (aspiration)

Tanmatras
Five Subtle Elements
Odor
Flavor
Visibility
Tangibility
Audibility

AUM
Pranava/Shabda

Atman
Indivisible Self

Kaivalya Prag-bhara

Ocean Of Consciousness
Brahman

"The classic and comprehensive meditation in Yoga and Vedanta dissolves the elements into the senses, the senses into the subtle elements, the subtle elements into the prana, the prana into the mind, the mind into the Great Mind, and the Great Mind into Om. Find Om in the Self, and dissolve that Self into the Great Self, Brahman."

Chart by Babaji Bob Kindler — Property of SRV Associates

getting into the eyes of all beings embodying in various realms. Not all can see or manage to actuate a purification process that will render a remedy for the dust of ignorance, providing a collyrium for the eyes that heals spiritual blindness. As Shankara has stated, *"The aspirant must keep the mirror of the mind polished daily with sadhana in order to maintain a vision of the Absolute that is free of overlays and mental imperfections."*

This is why the illumined souls come to earth in full recognition of the need to maintain a practice. Their true nature is perfect at all times, beyond time, but the mind they are about to invest that pure Consciousness in for purposes of embodiment is, number one, a mechanism, and number two, far from a perfect mechanism. Left devoid of attention and constant focus, it will accumulate cosmic dust like a ship's hull collects barnacles.

In chapter one, we studied the ascent of consciousness as it perceived, took account of, and connected four sets of fives to one another. Then we journeyed further inward by examining the prana and its subtle meaning. In the rest of the chapters the fourfold mind and the Cosmic Mind were both scrutinized and connected, using a host of teaching charts to help in the process. The Word was also taken up for contemplation, and many mentions of and teachings about the Self, *Atman*, were added in abundantly along the way.

Am I "That," or Not?

In the final foray through this chart we must begin as we are, Brahman, the Absolute. We are the Supreme Being pretending to single Itself out from the mass of Awareness without boundaries in order to descend to earth. For this It must undertake the sobering process of projecting the mindstream.

Before we embark from "On High" into the nether regions outside, it must be mentioned that there are a multitude of souls who have alienated themselves from the Absolute. Their consciousness is identified with matter, and has been for a score of lifetimes. When they depart Reality they fall into a dazed state from which they do not awaken, and then they emerge from the mother's womb in another body. This is root ignorance, the very epitomy of forgetfulness. As Ramprasad Sen sings, *"They give themselves to death, to the illusion of finitude."*

Sri Ramakrishna explains, *"The more that the embodied soul incarnates in ignorance, the more it begins to believe that the worlds of name and form are real, and that the soul is nonexistent."* Suffice to say that these beings are caught in the cosmic process for yugas, and on the lowest rungs of its cycles as well. Yet, as the Great Master also explained, *"If a man's mind gets boiled in the Fire of Knowledge, he will not be used thereafter for the new creation."* This rare yogic heat that saves comes from austerity, *tapas*. Tapas is a main facet of spiritual practice.

Souls on fire with higher wisdom, then, escape the cycles of birth and death in ignorance and attain to what Sri Krishna calls *"The worlds of no return."* Knowledge, and practice of its tenets, are really the main defining qualities for such attainment. As Sri Ramakrishna Paramahamsa states, again, *"The embodied soul at first remains in a state of ignorance. It is not conscious of God and oneness, but only of matter and multiplicity. It only notices the many things around it. Upon attaining knowledge it becomes conscious that God dwells in all beings. But on attaining higher wisdom it discards both knowledge and ignorance and talks of nothing but God day and night."*

Other than its many objects, part of the lure of the grosser realms of existence is the host of beings called ancestors. Here, on this earth, whole nations are found to be worshipping their ancestors. Worship is usually a good thing, but when it is stripped of the knowledge of celestials, gods and goddesses, illumined seers, and the Trinity – all higher and more powerful than ancestors – it falls short of any real benefit and can even cause crystallization and bondage. For the most part, what *Samsara* consists of is the constant return and exchange that goes on between the realm of the humans and the realm of the ancestors. Breaking this chain of cause and effect, like the Buddha did, ushers in the possibility of a greater freedom.

Emanation from the Source

The Soul, at the purest level, is *Brahman*. It is not individual anymore, but Indivisible. To explain this via visuals, the chart on the facing page lays out the process called *Chidabhasa*, how Brahman reflects Itself in and throughout the universes in space and time. This chart and its teachings will help us when the time comes to both project and dissolve the Mindstream.

Brahman, Absolute Reality, shines with pure Awareness. Its *Shakti* takes that incomparable sheen and emanates It as the rain of Intelligence into the Cosmic Mind. This deluge of Divinity passes through that sattvic mechanism and, as reflected consciousness, begins appearing as wisdom principles, cosmic laws, and subtle worlds in the rarest of ethers.

As this intelligent light of subtly conditioned awareness penetrates farther out into the *Lokas*, nourishing all the beings residing in those radiant climes, its vibratory rate changes as it fashions the collective and individual mind with living intelligence. Celestial realms, lower life-heavens, and prana-laced atmospheres form by its blissful presence, and finally the worlds of solid mass appear, congealed by the individual and collective mind's brooding on subtle senses and subtle elements. The physical body is next, created in order to house the five gross senses for the purpose of enjoying the sense objects.

This entire trickle-down process really kicks in when the Cosmic Mind, *Mahat*, gets ahold of the *Mahashakti's* amassed wisdom rays and begins to "stream" them in a sequence – a sequence that does not end, not even when objects are broken down into tiny particles vibrating too swiftly to comprehend. The ego-mind mechanism – from the celestials and ancestors on down to humankind – loves this endless display, and thrives on its constant permutations. This is really addiction to prana rather than its mastery.

But to reverse this marvelous projection is the real joy, for it leads to Bliss and Life Eternal rather than to stale preoccupation with unreal materials and decaying bodies. The soul that can perceive the hidden workings beyond matter, cause and

Chidabhasa — The Reflection of Brahman in the Cosmos

"God is not in the universe; the universe is in God." Swami Vivekananda

BRAHMAN — ABSOLUTE REALITY

(Maha Shakti)

Direct Emanation of Pure Conscious Awareness

(Atman)   (Unmanifest Prakriti)

BUDDHI — COSMIC INTELLIGENCE

Chidabhasa
(Reflected Consciousness)

Brahmajnan Appearing as Various Eternal Principles

Prana & Akasha
Subtle Energy,
The Subtle Worlds,
Higher Gradated Beings

Human Ego-Mind Complex
Thought, Conceptualization,
Visions, Imagination,
Projection, Invention, Desire

Time & Space
Five Subtle Elements,
Five Gross Elements.
Physical Universe,
Flow of Events, Karma

Human Embodiment
The Body,
Five Senses of Knowledge,
Five Senses of Action

"The embodied being is none other than an emanation of the Jnana-wisdom of Brahman. The hosts of myriad worlds and objects appearing within endless cycles of time duly shine as the objective vision and ideation of its inherent Consciousness. Thus, it is the one, all-pervading Atman which assumes the name of "Jiva," materializing with the intelligent force of its own innate Awareness." Lord Vasishtha

effect style, and meditate on each facet of existence in order to gain control over the mind's relationship with them, courts a freedom scarcely imagined by the greater percentage of living beings occupying most of the realms of name and form.

"Brh," From Brahman — "To Expand"

"The Lord verily breathed upon the Waters of Existence," *"Suddenly there was Light in the Darkness,"* *"The One decided: 'I will become Many'"* — however the seers and the scriptures might venture to explain it, the process of cosmic evolution is a mighty undertaking, and an important topic. That the Nondual Reality expands, or turns itself into the many, is a concept that nondual philosophers of India would not accept.

That is why there is a level of philosophy called Qualified Nondualism. It avers, as Sri Ramakrishna has stated, that *"God has become all this — the world and its living beings."* The homogeneity of existence may be the highest Truth, but embodied beings, mainly due to belief in their own sense of separateness, cannot comprehend it yet, and most cannot even admit it. The idea of expansion, or evolution, makes them more comfortable.

For the rare intrepid spiritual soul, however, change takes place only in nature, never in Reality. Brahman does not transform — *aparinama* — and this is the barometer that measures spiritual realization among the sages and seers. The *Dissolution of the Mindstream* practice, then, is the last bit of change and transformation, the last trace of process, that the soul will undertake. Let us enter into it here, so that the meditator will gain an advantage in his or her personal meditations at home, in the temple, or in the shrine room.

Ecstatic Projection and Its Sacrifices

Referring back to the main chart on page 85, as well as on page 3, we will begin in Brahman as the ever free, never bound Soul Essence that we are — *Atman*. Countless souls who have accomplished successful *Dissolution of the Mindstream* are flowing into Brahman along a mighty river of Consciousness known well to illumined souls, called *Kaivalya Prag-bhara*.

Into that radiant stream, in reverse fashion and against the tide of merging souls, we emanate down as sentient wisdom-rays, entering next into that pool of pure potential called The Word. AUM is reverberating there, the ecstatic sound of divine generation, like the hum of a thousand bumble bees circling a massive hive of honey.

Just being, and storing up power, we gradually become aware of an all-pervasive Overseeress who is tending that hive of pure potential. In the next timeless moment, we are aware of a circular opening to Light, an outward moving channel in The Word that both emits and absorbs simultaneously. With the subtle inward power of soul-projection, we move towards that aperture, instantly recognizing it as the "Wisdom Eye." Through that scintillating opening we pass, finding ourselves in the sweet and balanced region of *Mahat*, known to illumined souls also as *Hiranyagarbha*. We have penetrated the Cosmic Egg.

The Mahat is warm and welcoming. A triple force dwells in It. We recognize It due to teachings from the gurus over millennia, and therefore bow with reverence to the Lords of Projection, Sustenance, and Withdrawal – Brahman, Vishnu, and Siva.

With their permission we take leave and, borrowing the powers of Causality from Them, and recounting the cosmic laws in memory, formulate the sheath of mind and intellect for inhabitation. Giving up, with difficulty, the unbounded freedom we have enjoyed up to this point, we fashion a separate state of awareness necessary for entering the grosser realms of name and form. That condition, called *ahamkara*, immediately begins to endear itself to us, partially obliterating the sweet bliss of oneness we are leaving behind.

Before us is a stream of intelligence, far less intense than the one we viewed earlier, where souls were entering into Brahman. Our causal memory informs us that this is the Chitta, or at least the higher end of it, for far below, as it were, we see an infinite set of flows that are the various thought-streams emanating from many beings abiding in different realms of awareness. We now recall the Life-heavens, and make ready to encounter them – all within our own awareness.

As if by appearance due to the mere thought of it, the psychic prana unveils itself, flowing like a stream all its own towards realms where the Light we have heretofore been constantly aware of is diminishing and fading fast. Nevertheless, we merge with the flow of prana and free fall towards the realm of solidity.

As we descend, we can detect how thought begins to congeal in order to fashion this physical loka. Remembering the gift of the Mahat, we take stock of the subtle power of all-pervasiveness, homogeneity, luminosity, liquidity, and solidity – in that order – and begin to connect those five with the existence of three other sets of fives that are fast approaching. This is hard work, but exceedingly crucial; for losing sight of these connections, or losing them entirely, will result in forgetfulness and disorientation. What is more, it is all happening very swiftly. Thus, it becomes apparent to us at this juncture how souls get born and reborn, bereft of both the knowledge of the inner terrain of their own consciousness, and stripped of the recognition of their Divine Self as well.

A mass of embodied beings now spreads out across the scope of our inner vision. We see them engaged in a multitude of preoccupations, most of them oblivious to anything other than the materials that surround them. They are hemmed in by them, these objects, and are doting on them as if they were existence itself.

Putting this strange phenomena aside for the moment, our immediate attention is drawn to those human couples who are engaged in acts of procreation. Birth in the realm of the Bhutakasha will require a physical body, a prospect that is undesirable but necessary. Several factors accost us at this point in time, which is rapidly slowing down now, allowing for choices.

First, there is the choice of timing, very important in order to avoid being subject to the formation of the fetus and the gestation period in the body of the human female. Arriving into the infant stage of life just prior to the newborn's ejection from the womb is an art of incarnation, though some beings will meditate in that state sometime prior to birth.

Secondly, there is the matter of choosing ideal parents, as well as the choice of gender. During the inspection period, prior to embodiment, the aware soul had already found the parents it would select, based upon inherent qualities that would provide a fitting atmosphere for remaining conscious of the Soul, exposure to the teachings of the dharma, and acquiring the ability to transmit these teachings to others. The enlightened soul knows there are no other reasons than these to embody, or, that all other purposes will be satisfied when these three are present.

Identifying temporarily with the power of the subtle senses, we now inject the newfound body with all the potential of primal connections. Though still new and underdeveloped, all the forces of the ten gross senses are suddenly upon us. We are invested with eyes to see light, lungs to breathe air, ears to hear sounds, and the ability of touch in a new world. Odors suggest themselves early on, and nourishment is already being provided at the mother's breast. Liquids, solid things, light and darkness, inspiration and helplessness — all of these and more are being experienced in rapid, cyclic fashion. Awareness, coming and going as sleep and waking, takes us over.

But over and above all of this, a divine atmosphere still prevails, a tangible Light that those now around us obviously cannot see. The illumined soul taking on the body will retain the vision of this Light throughout life, hiding it away and bringing it forward at various junctures in life.

And this facility is mainly due to the luminary's implementation of the power of dissolution, the twin ability to both remember the source of origin, and return to It as well. It takes practice at first, as with any ability, but it soon becomes natural. As the Holy Mother, Sri Sarada Devi, once told us: *"I can take my Atman out from hiding and gaze at It anytime I like, just as easily as you might look at a fruit in the palm of your hand."*

The Benefits of the Dissolution of the Mindstream

For embodied beings, at least those who enter into physical manifestation with their mental and spiritual capacities intact, the *Dissolution of the Mindstream* ability is a priceless treasure. If one took the advice of the luminaries around this matter, they would simply say, "Don't leave home without it." But for the spiritual aspirant, learning the technique for this ability is even more important, for if the Mindstream can effectively be dissolved, so too will all the defects in the mind disappear.

Finally, even learning about the existence of such a principle will begin to inform the novice of an entire realm of existence that he or she is not yet aware of. Taken at face value, there is hardly a more thorough and effective practice available and, as we have seen throughout the pages and teachings placed in the content of this book, the *Dissolution of the Mindstream* is really what is taking place at the foundation of all other practices associated with spiritual life and its salient aims and ends.

Reverse the Process

For the practitioner of meditation, the daily exercise of withdrawing the mind from objects, called *pratyahara* in Yoga, is necessary — even for one's very peace of mind, what to speak of gaining Enlightenment.

At first, in the early stages of awakening to the subtle truths of one's being, the problems of brooding, worry, restlessness of mind, and other aberrations of the thought process may intrude. But this is all the more reason to master the mind's tendency to flow outwards only, whether that flow is erratic and haphazard as with the rajasic mind, or weak and nonproductive as in the case of the tamasic mind.

In either case, or in the event that the mind has already gained power but needs control, focus, and direction, the inward coursing of its constant stream of thought along pathways already described herein will keep it from evils such as materialism, worldliness, complacency, jadedness, and of course, ignorance of its true nature.

Moreover, coming to perceive and familiarize itself with the internal realms of consciousness at all levels and stations will make an indelible impression upon it, a *samskara* that will assist it in remembering the cosmos at its three levels — gross, subtle, and causal (or waking, dreaming, and deep sleep).

Otherwise, and devoid of this singular meditative ability, samskaras, mental impressions caused by external actions, will deposit their residue and leave their mark on the soul, causing a chain of rebirths based upon what is external alone. This is called the lack of a spiritual life, what Jesus saw among the fishermen when he first came upon them along the river. To make them effective *"fishers of men"* he had to encourage them to get an inner life of the Spirit by informing them of the *"Kingdom of Heaven"* within and the *All-Mighty Father.*

Some Dangers of Formless Meditation

Formless meditation, for the adept, is a great and wondrous thing. But how many adepts of it do we find in this day and time, in our materialistic societies? To jump in one's meditation practice from the physical world to Nondual Reality in one leap is not only practically impossible, but quite inadvisable as well. That is why the great founders of the world's religions and teachers alike advise meditation on God with form, initially.

And here is where the *Dissolution of the Mindstream* affords the gradual inward ascension so crucial for comprehensive realization. As the Father of Yoga taught, the meditator can begin by concentrating on earth, water, fire, air, and ether, as *alambamas*. Alambanas are foundations for meditation, much like the *pratika* or *pratima* advised in early Vedantic and Buddhist meditations, i.e., such objects as a stone obelisk, a picture of a luminary, or a candle flame in a windless place. The mind stills and gets peaceful and steady via such early forays into the nature of existence, even at its gross level. *"Meditate on that which is pleasing to the mind,"* as the Father of Yoga has put it. He also states, *"When the fivefold perceptions of Yoga rising from concentration on earth, water, light, air, and ether have appeared to the yogin, then he gains a body consisting of the fire of Yoga, and he will never again be touched by disease, old age, and death."*

Even if the venturesome meditator is able to attain some formless samadhi, and even if he can hold it and get something definitive from it before the door to formlessness closes, possibly for months or years, the intermediate realms of existence remain virtually unknown to him. Everything from the prana that is carrying his consciousness towards formlessness, on through to the lokas of the ancestors and celestials, and even the important and beneficial realms and bardos of the benign and wrathful deities, simply escapes his awareness.

This one-sided dimension of meditation and meditator is verily ineffective for such things as departing the body in full awareness at the time of death, returning to earth consciously (as in the cases of the *jivanmuktas* and *bodhisattvas*), and teaching other beings the steps and stages to their Enlightenment. Comprehension of all levels of awareness, and comprehensive knowledge of all that resides within them, is what is called for in authentic spiritual life and realization. Seeing the trend away from such all-embracing inclusion, Swami Vivekananda stated: *"Would to God that all men were so constituted that in their minds all of these elements — philosophy, mysticism, emotion, and work — were equally present in full! That is the ideal, my ideal of a perfect man. Everyone who has only one or two of these elements I consider one-sided; and this world is almost full of such 'one-sided' men, with knowledge of that one road only in which they move."*

Masterful Mind Dissolution

To master a thing, thought, problem, or principle is to know it via study and meditation and thereby overcome all fear associated with it. This is the criterion for consummate knowledge. Simply storing surface information in the mind's memory will not amount to anything really beneficial. A case in point, is that when the modern mind knows a thing on the intellectual level only, without having meditated upon its true nature, the thought of it will persist in the mind, not dissolve, and brooding will then take place, not peace. Fear of said issue, of reprisal, or, to put it plainly, of karmic repercussions, will remain. Even what is pleasurable and satisfying to the mind will be attended with fear of losing those feelings. True knowledge, then, is based in renunciation, not ownership, and brings destruction of fear, not mere repetition of past experiences.

Siddhanta – One's Own Final Conclusion

The practitioner of the *Dissolution of the Mindstream* method will sit daily and take the time to direct attention to the levels of his or her own consciousness that are listed on the main chart of this book. From the elements, to the senses, to contemplation of the life-force, and further inward still, his own mind will soon come under his control and reveal to him the eternal worlds within. Knowing these, he will merely follow the Light that is reflected in them to its Source, and merge therein. This inner movement is blissful, unattended by fear, because knowledge of all things has rid him of fear forever. As Sri Krishna states in the Bhagavad Gita, *"For that one who is poised in Yoga, his mind becomes his own friend, but to the one whose mind is restless and uncontrolled, that very mind becomes his enemy."*

The entire process of *Dissolving the Mindstream* can be described in one paragraph, which is inscribed at the bottom of the main chart we have been examining:

"The classic and comprehensive meditation in Yoga and Vedanta dissolves the elements into the senses, the senses into the subtle elements, the subtle elements into the prana, the prana into the mind, the mind into the Great Mind, and the Great Mind into Om. Find Om in the Self, and dissolve that Self into the Great Self, Brahman." Om Peace, Peace, Peace.

Sanskrit Glossary

Acharyas — Great teachers, usually appearing as the heads in charge of entire lineages.

Adhyasa — False reflection occuring due to the superimposition of attributes of one thing over another.

Advaitic — Referring to Advaita, the nondualistic philosophy of the Vedanta.

Advaitists — Those who follow Advaita philosophy.

Ahamkara — Ego, not so much as a personality or an attitude, but as a principle which causes the sense of separation of the embodied soul from formless Awareness.

Ajati — Unborn; free of caste and species.

Akasha — Space, atmosphere, of which there are five — Bhutakasha (space of objects); Pranakasha (space of lifeforce or vital energy); Chittakasha (space of mentation); Jnanakasha (space of intelligence); Chidakasha (space of Consciousness).

Alambanas — Foundations for meditation, which can range from anything from the five elements to Cosmic Mind and Ishvara.

Amrita — Nectar, meaning the Nectar of Wisdom indicating Eternal Life.

Ananda — The unalloyed, uninterrupted Bliss of Awareness.

Ananda Ghana — Mass of Bliss, meaning Brahman, the Absolute.

Anatman — The nonself; the human ego complex.

Antahkarana — The Fourfold Mind complex, consisting of manas, buddhi, chitta, and ahamkara.

Antaryami — The "Inner Ruler Immortal seated in the Heart"; Atman; Witness Consciousness.

Aparinama — Nontransformation, describing the perfect and changeless nature of Brahman.

Aparokshanubhuti — One's own direct spiritual experience which also provides the proof of all dharmic teachings.

Arsha-Bhasha — The ancient Sanskrit language used by the seers of Truth.

Asamprajnata — Seedless Samadhi in Yoga, meaning formless, correlative with the Nirvikalpa of Vedanta.

Asamvedana — A refined spiritual quality of the adept that allows for complete transparency of mind; imperishable Jnana.

Asparsha — Untouched, undefiled, referring to the Yoga of transcendance.

Asteya — Nonstealing, or noncovetousness, which is one of the five yamas of Yoga.

Atma Vichara — In-depth introspection of the nature of the true Self of human beings.

Atmic — Having to do with the Atman, the Supreme Soul of man.

AUM — The sacred syllable of Brahman.

Avatar — Literally, "That which Descends," referring to the Divine Incarnations of God who embody on earth to help souls.

Avatars — Divine Incarnations, of which there is but one, but who takes various forms from age to age.

Avarana — Veiling power of Maya that obscures Reality.

Avidya — Ignorance of one's divine nature as formless Essence.

Bardo — A measure of time and space in which events take place, even before embodiment and after disembodiment.

Bhagavad Gita — The sacred wisdom song of Sri Krishna, which is one of the three most hallowed scriptures in Indian religious tradition.

Bhurloka — The realm of physical objects, and the first of seven inward-reaching levels of consciousness, and the plane of physical beings — humans, animals, insects, and plants — corresponding to the Muladhara chakra.

Bhutakasha — The realm or space of physically manifested beings.

Bhutas — Physcial beings; manifested objects; disembodied spirits; any of the five elements.

Bhuvarloka — The realm of heaven proper, the second of seven inward-reaching levels of Consciousness, corresponding to the Svadhisthana chakra, wherein reside the ancestors, celestials, siddhas, and munis.

Bodhisattvas — Beings who take vows of loyalty that bring them to earth for a series of lifetimes in order to help others reach the enlightened state.

Brahma — The Lord of Creation who projects the worlds at the time of new beginnings or cosmic cycles.

Brahmakaravrittidhyana — The formless meditation on Reality that stills all the thought vibrations of the mind.

Brahmaloka — The seventh and highest of the seven inward-reaching realms of Consciousness (which correspond with the seven chakras). Consciousness here is scarcely in a "state," or "center," or "realm," but is closest to Its pristine condition as formless Awareness.

Brahman — Nameless, Formless, Reality, i.e., God.

Buddhi — Higher Intelligence, to be distinguished from the mental buddhi as the intellectual sheath which contains intelligence.

Chaitanya — Pure, conscious Awareness, which is Supreme Reality in Indian religion and philosophy.

Chakras — Spiritual centers, or vortexes, which receive and conduct Kundalini Shakti.

Chid — Pure, conscious Awareness.

Chidabhasa — The reflection of Reality in relativity.

Chidakasha — The boundless space of pure, conscious Awareness.

Chitta — "Stuff of the mind," meaning its thoughts, concepts, content, projections, imaginings, etc.

Chittakasha — The inner space of mind and thoughts, aligned collectively and cosmically with the highest heavens, beginning with the gods and goddesses and ascending inwardly to the sages.

Darshanas — Paths of clear seeing, referring to the Six Orthodox Darshanas of India — Sankhya, Nyaya, Vaisheshika, Yoga, Purva Mimamsa, and Uttara Mimamsa (Vedanta); attending upon a holy person for spiritual instruction.

Desha — Space, along with kala, time, and nimitta, causality.

Devas — The gods, or "shining ones," inhabiting realms higher and subtler than that of the ancestors and celestials.

Devi — The Goddess, the "devis" if She appears in Her many aspects.

Dhammapada — The scripture of original Buddhism, consisting of teachings of the Buddha gathered by the Arhats of the tradition after his passing into Samadhi.

Dharana — Concentration, which is the sixth of the eight limbs of traditional Yoga (Patanjala); a particular yoga of the Divine Mother path.

Dharma — Divine Life, lived in accordance and observation of the precepts, laws, and axioms of dharma.

Dharmic — Having to do with the dharma and its influence.

Dasabhumikas — The ten pure lands of the Buddhist Bodhisattva.

Dhyana — Meditation proper, which is the seventh of eight limbs of traditional Yoga.

Gunas — The three gunas of *tamas, rajas,* and *sattva* which correspond to the principles of lassitude, restlessness, and balance in the human mind. All three, even balance (sattva), are to be transcended, as their presence signals the disequilibrium which ushers in the worlds of name and form in time and space.

Garuda — The powerful dragon bird who is Lord Vishnu's mount, representing the prana that carries consciousness from realm to realm, state to state.

Guru — Spiritual preceptor, whose grace and aid are indispensible for successful spiritual life.

Hatha — A school of Yoga focused on body postures and breathing exercises, whose original purpose was to strengthen the body and purify the nervous system so as to help make them fit for spiritual life and meditation. In later centuries, and especially in present times, the system's aims have degraded into the search for bodily health, occult powers, and longevity. As Svatmarama states in his *Hatha Yoga Pradipika* (16th century), "*Raja Yoga begins where Hatha Yoga leaves off.*"

Hathis — Those who follow the hatha yoga path, seeking health, longevity, and occult powers via physical asana and pranayam.

Hiranyagarbha — The Cosmic Egg, or Golden Egg, often perceived as one or similar with the Cosmic Mind or Mahat, Unmanifested Prakriti, and even AUM. Anthropomorphically, it corresponds directly with Lord Brahma of the Hindu Trinity.

Indus River — One of India's seven sacred rivers, present at the earliest period in Indian history, and associated with the Himalayas and the enlightened luminaries.

Ishavasyopanisad — One of the 108 Upanisads making up the sacred scriptures of India, it is one of the major ones commented on by Shankara during his lifetime.

Ishtam — The Chosen Ideal upon whom the devotee meditates in the shrine of the heart, realizing an ineffable Presence in deepest contemplation.

Ishvara — Same as Ishtam, and referring to the Divine Personality of God with form; one of the five seats of the Devi.

Ishvari — The Divine Personality in feminine form.

Iti Iti — Literally, "All this, All this," referring to the realization that "All is Brahman," attained after practicing the discipline of Neti Neti, "Not this, Not this."

Jagad — The physical world.

Jagrat — The first of four states of a human being's awareness, that of waking consciousness.

Janaloka — The realm of the great spiritual beings, the fifth of seven inward-reaching levels of Consciousness, corresponding with the fifth chakra, the Vishuddha.

Jiva — The embodied soul.

Jivanmuktas — Those liberated beings, having gotten freedom while in the body, who then embody and reflect the highest state of Awareness for other beings.

Jivatman — The Atman existing in the form of the embodied soul, but as yet unrealized.

Jnana — Wisdom, specifically of the spiritual type.

Jnana Chakshu — Another name for the Third Eye; sixth chakra.

Jnanakasha — The space of Intelligence, it is the fourth akasha, or space of consciousness, and corresponds with the realm of the seers and luminaries.

Jnanendriyas — The five organs of knowledge, i.e., hearing, touching, seeing, tasting, and smelling.

Kaivalya-prag-bhara — The stream of souls who have gained liberation from form and are flowing towards immersion in Brahman.

Kala — Time; a name for Siva.

Kalas — Phases of time, being one of the cosmic laws.

Kalachakra — The wheel of birth and death suffered in ignorance.

Kaivalya — Isolation; in Yoga, the penultimate aim of separation of the Soul from nature.

Kamalakanta — A devotee of Mother Kali whose sacred devotional wisdom songs inspired Sri Ramakrishna and all of Bengal.

Kapila — The revered systematizer of the Sankhya philosophy.

Karana — Cause; the name of the third body of the non-Self of man, the other two being gross and subtle — Sthula and Sukshma.

Karmendriyas — The five organs of action, i.e., speaking, acting, locomotion, procreation, and excretion.

Karmic — Anything having to do with cause and effect, but particularly with the repercussions from good and bad actions done.

Klesha — An impediment in Yoga, like egoism and ignorance.

Klistha — Pain-bearing, referring to those negative thoughts that bring suffering on oneself and others.

Kundalini — Literally, "coiled up," referring to the spiritual potential in mankind which lies dormant in the Muladhara Chakra.

Kurukshetra — The battlefield upon which Sri Krishna transmitted the wisdom of Vedanta to Arjuna during the war between the Pandava and Kaurava clans.

Layachintayadhyana — The meditation that dissolves all things into Brahman, in three stages, culminating in total immersion.

Linga — The root syllable of Lord Siva called "sva," which dwells in the Svadhisthana Chakra; in Yoga, a designation of all that is "marked" with form, as opposed to what is alinga, "unmarked" or formless; another name of rhe sukshma sharira, or subtle body.

Loka — A realm of existence, which, unlike the physical planets in outer space, exist within, and which are gradated into various levels that host ancestral, celestial, subtle, and causal beings.

Lokas — A collection of internal realms.

Mahabhutas — The five elements: earth, water, fire, air, and ether.

Mahamaya — Literally, "Supreme Maya"; a powerful name for the

Divine Mother of the Universe, which points to Her as the overseeress of all of Existence.

Maharloka — The fourth of the internal realms of existence which corresponds with the Anahata Chakra of the Kundalini system.

Mahaprakriti — The Divine Mother as She presides over gross, subtle, and causal nature; Unmanifested Nature.

Mahashakti — Literally, "Great Shakti," which is a name for the Divine Mother of the Universe as the pervading intelligent power in all things, all beings.

Mahat — Referring to the Great Mind, or God's Mind, which in the Sankhya Yoga system is the causal hub of all that is formless, and which later gets projected into form.

Mahavidya — Literally, "Great Wisdom," signifying the Mother of all Wisdom who fashions worlds out of living Intelligence.

Manojavittvam — Amazing speed of the mind, one of the seven victories in Tantra.

Mantras — A collection of Sanskrit word formulas which aid the Vedic priest in performing worship, and which help the spiritual aspirant purify, refine, and clarify the mind, preparing it for samadhi.

Matras — Quintessential particles, especially those consisting of meaning and intelligence found in sacred words, scripture, and mind.

Maya — The worlds of name and form in time and space based in causation.

Mayic — Of, about, or referring to anything that is of the realm of name and form in time and space, based in causation — Maya.

Mithya — False, having to do mainly with deluded thinking.

Moksha — A state of freedom always at hand; for the soul caught in the illusion of finitude, it is liberation from all bondage.

Mundakopanisad — One of the 108 Upanisads making up the sacred scriptures of India, it is one of the major ones commented on by Shankara during his lifetime.

Mudha — Foolish, dull.

Mukhyaprana — The essential constituent in the five forms of prana which, when flowing, conduces to perfect health in the body. This health, gotten from taking sanctified food with a reverential attitude, is a sign that the mukhyaprana is ready to be refined via spiritual disciplines and transformed into Ojas.

Mukti — Liberation, or the state of freedom always at hand.

Mulavidya — Root ignorance; primal ignorance.

Muni — A wise being, sagelike in understanding.

Nadi — A subtle nerve which conducts pranic energy and, when purified, acts to carry spiritual vibrations as well.

Nadis — The overall network of thousands of subtle nerves running through the human body/mind mechanism.

Neti Neti — "Not this, Not this," referring to that practice that the aspirant does in order to rid the mind of all that is not Real.

Nimitta — Causality, or Causation, being one of the cosmic laws.

Nirguna — Free of attributes, as in Nirguna Brahman.

Nirvana — State of total absorption into Reality, like Nirvikalpa.

Nirvichara Samadhi — Samadhi free of mental vibrations and intellectual inquiry.

Nirvikalpa — Literally, "beyond all thought-forms" including time, equating to the deepest formless samadhi, nondual in essence.

Nirvitarka Samadhi — Samadhi free of logic and intellectualization.

Nivritti — Withdrawing from worldly existence; renunciation.

Niyamas — The five preliminary spiritual observances – purity, contentedness, study of scriptures, austerity, and devotion to God – practiced by the aspirant of classic Yoga prior to sitting (asana) and breathing exercises (pranayama); also, the ten niyamas of Tantra.

Ojas — The spiritual power which culminates as a result of comingling the ingestion of sanctified food with recitation of mantra, heightened vital energy, and spiritual disciplines.

Om — Same as AUM, the most sacred bijam or seed syllable, which is seen as the Word of Brahman sporting a myriad of connotations and blessings.

Omkara — Om, or AUM, as the cause of all manifestation.

Panchamahabhutas — The five elements.

Param — Supreme.

Paramahamsa — "Great Swan," a name for a unique type of illumined soul who is simultaneously a superlative teacher and a past master of spirituality.

Paramatman — The supreme Soul, unique in comparison to its lesser manifestations such as the Jivatman.

Paravidya — Higher knowledge, spiritual wisdom of revealed scripture and direct spiritual experience – as contrasted to ordinary (dualistic) scripture and intellectual knowledge (aparavidya).

Patanjali — The founder, father, or systematizer of the classic Yoga of Patanjala.

Prajnaparam — Supreme Intelligence, which was a name that Lord Buddha used for Formless Reality.

Prakriti — Nature, both manifested and unmanifested, which is insentient as opposed to Purusha, the Sentient Self or Soul.

Pralaya — The withdrawal of all form into abeyance at the time of final dissolution.

Prana — Life force, referring to the subtle energy that, among other things, not only affords the physical body its existence and operations, but also functions as the vital energy that sustains and lifts thoughts, and carries beings out of the body at the time of passing.

Pranakasha — The space of vital force, or prana, which corresponds with the realm of the ancestors.

Pranava — Another designation for Om, signifying it as the origin of prana in all its forms.

Pranayama — Specialized breathing exercises in Yogic practice which help the aspirant recognize the pervasive nature of prana and bring it under control for the purpose of purification of mind and Self-realization.

Pranic — About or having to do with prana.

Pratika — A symbol for God used in worship.

Pratima — An object used in early meditative practice to help the mind gain focus.

Pratyahara — The fifth limb of Yoga that demands the withdrawal of the mind from all objects, outer and inner.

Puranas — Secondary scriptures of India, as contrasted to the primary scriptures such as the Upanisads and Bhagavad Gita.

Purnyata — Fullness, indicating the complete and comprehensive nature of Divine Reality.

Raja Yoga — Another name for Patanjala, or Ashtanga Yoga.

Rajas — One of the three gunas, or modes of nature, signifying energy in nature and restlessness in the mind.

Rajasic — Being overcome or influenced with action or restlessness.

Ramakrishna — A spiritual luminary of 19th century Bengal who is considered by many to be the Avatar of the Kali Yuga.

Ramprasad Sen — A celebrated Bengali poet/saint of India.

Rishis — Illumined souls of the Vedic period in India who were seers of the Truth, and whose descendants distilled the ancient wisdom into sacred texts like the Upanisads.

Sadhana — Specialized spiritual exercises and disciplines which qualify the sincere aspirant for awakening to the presence of the chakras in the gross, subtle, and causal bodies, all leading to realization of nondual Truth and samadhi.

Sadhaka — A seeker of spirituality, one who engages in sadhana, spiritual discipline.

Sahasranama — The thousand Names, meaning any of a host of such lists which are chanted in propitiation of various deities.

Saguna — Accompanied by attributes, as in Saguna Brahman, God with Form.

Samadhana — Focused meditation; one of the Six Jewels of Vedanta.

Samadhi — Any of a host of rare spiritual experiences, usually of the wisdom variety but not exclusive of devotional bhavas and moods, wherein the practitioner beholds levels of inner consciousness leading up and into the nondual state.

Samprajnata Samadhi — All the samadhis of Yoga which fall within the realm of form; seeded samadhis.

Samskaras — An important word in Sanskrit and Indian philosophy referring to impressions left in the mind by repetitive past actions, which, in the case of negative impressions, and when left unneutralized, cause the transmigrating soul (mind complex) to be born again and again in Samsara.

Sananda Samadhi — The samadhi of Yoga which is still attended by individual bliss, i.e., not yet formless or nondual.

Sangha — A group of spiritually-minded devotees and practitioners.

Sankalpa — The vibrational activity of the mind complex which sets in motion worlds in space and time, all projected at the cosmic, collective, and individual levels in conjunction with one another.

Sankhya — One of the Six Orthodox Darshanas, the most ancient Indian Philosophy that influenced all that came after it based mainly upon its rendering of the Twenty-four Cosmic Principles.

Sanskrit — The ancient and timeless language of Mother India, holding the potential for transmitting deep spiritual truths that are generally missing in other languages.

Sharira — Covering; sheath; body.

Sarvosmi — A one-word Mahavakya meaning, "Everything Is."

Sasmita Samadhi — The samadhi of Yoga which is still attended by the sense of ego, therefore not yet formless or nondual.

Satchidananda — One of the divine names for God in India, meaning Pure Existence, Pure Knowledge, and Pure Bliss.

Satsanga — A gathering of beings who seek Truth first and foremost, and who search for answers to issues and concerns inhibiting Its manifestation and expression.

Sattva — One of the three gunas of nature, signifying balance in nature and happiness in the mind.

Sattva-Purusha-Nytakhyati — Supreme Mastery; the highest of the Seven Victories in Tantra.

Satya — Truthfulness; one of the five yamas of Yoga.

Savichara Samadhi — A samadhi of Yoga which is attended by reasoning and deliberation.

Savikalpa Samadhi — Conditioned Samadhi of Vedanta, as contrasted to Nirvikalpa which is unconditioned.

Savitarka Samadhi — A samadhi of Yoga which is accompanied by intellectual rationalization and argumentation.

Shabda — Another designation for AUM.

Shakta — A follower of the Divine Mother and Her pathways.

Shakti — Dynamic spiritual energy.

Shaktis — Any of a host of powers emanating off of the Divine Mother of the Universe, the main four of which are Iccha (will), Jnana (wisdom), Kriya (spontaneous action), and Dravya (creativity).

Shankara — The great Advaitin whose scriptures and commentaries figure as one of the highest authorities in Vedanta philosophy.

Shankaracharya — Same as Shankara, with the addition "acharya" designating him as a great teacher.

Shanti — Peace, usually referred to as the peace of equanimity.

Shatavadana — One of the Evolutes of Maya, it means thinking a thousand things at once, indicating a scattered mind.

Shiva — Same as Siva.

Shraddha — Faith.

Shravana — Hearing the Truth, which is the first of the three Proofs of Truth.

Shruti — Scripture of the most authoritative kind, superior to Smriti and Itihasa; to be heard.

Shunyata — Emptiness, meaning the realization of the lack of any real abiding essence in names and forms, in relativity.

Siddhanta — A philosophical conclusion that allows for spiritual progress.

Siddhas — As in the eight occult powers, called Astabalasiddhas, which lead the aspirant away from the goal of spiritual life.

Siva — The Lord of Wisdom, and third of the Hindu Trinity of primary Deities; one of the five seats of the Devi.

Slokas — Statements which make up a scripture.

Smritibedu — Causal memory, such as of one's previous births.

Spandas — Internal vibrational fields of awareness, like realms or lokas.

Sphota — The Manifestor; an appellation for The Word, AUM.

Sri Aurobindo — An important spiritual figure in the spreading of Vedic Wisdom in the twentieth century, and the author of many inspiring books on spirituality.

Sri Sarada Devi — The revered and blessed wife and spiritual consort of Sri Ramakrishna Paramahamsa, believed by thousands of living beings to be the Incarnation of the Divine Mother in this age. She was confirmed by Sri Ramakrishna to be an incarnation of the Goddesses Kali, Lakshmi, and Sarasvati conjoined.

Srimad Devi Bhagavatam — One of a few quintessential Mother scriptures of India, and the most authoritative text of the Shakti tradition.

Sthiti Samadhi — A state of steady samadhi.

Sthiti — Steadiness.

Sthula — Gross, meaning apparent, not subtle; one of the three bodies of mankind, namely gross, subtle, and causal.

Sukshma — Subtle; one of the three bodies of mankind, namely gross, subtle, and causal (sthula, sukshma, and karana).

Sukshmadhyana — Meditation on the subtle truths found in the scriptures.

Sukshma Sharira — The subtle body of mankind, the fourfold mental vehicle.

Sushumna — The "central channel" along which are arranged the seven chakras of Kundalini, and around which circle the Ida and Pingala nadis.

Sushupti — Deep sleep state, often correlated with formlessness, and the "M" of AUM.

Sutra — A Sanskrit verse, as in the Yoga Sutras.

Svadhisthana chakra — The second chakra, associated in physical terms with the region of the sexual organs, but specifically aligned inwardly with the realm of Bhuvarloka.

Svadhyaya — Study, recitation, and memorization of scripture as a prerequisite to other spiritual practices like asana and pranayam, and pratyahara. It is one of the ten yamas and niyamas of traditional Yoga (Patanjala).

Svaha — A designation for the third loka, or Svarloka, it is also a pronouncement of auspiciousness used in ceremonial worship.

Svapna — The dream state, or second of mankind's three states of consciousness (waking, dreaming, and deep sleep), associated with the "U" of AUM.

Svarloka — The realm of higher heavens, and the third of seven inward-reaching levels of consciousness which sport deities, celestials, noble ancestors, and those beings who gather around them — corresponding to the Manipura chakra.

Svarupa — Essence, meaning pure Consciousness or Awareness.

Svarupadhyana — Meditation on one's own Essence, or Atman.

Svetashvatara — The name of one of the more recent Upanisads, containing teachings of powerful merit and boundless scope.

Swami — The title given to monks of the Hindu religion who have taken monastic vows and received authority to teach spirituality to others.

Swami Aseshananda — The last living monastic disciple of Sri Sarada Devi up until his passing in the 1990's.

Swami Sivananda — One of the sixteen direct disciples of Sri Ramakrishna Paramahamsa.

Swami Vivekananda — The foremost of the direct disciples of Sri Ramakrishna Paramahamsa, who brought the Vedanta to the West in 1893, and became known as the World Teacher.

Tailadharadhyana — The meditation that proceeds from the flow of unbroken concentration from the human mind, to the receptacle of the boundless Brahman.

Tamas — One of the three gunas, or modes of nature, signifying inertia in nature and slothfulness in the mind.

Tamasic — Being under the influence or control of sloth or torpor.

Tanmatra — Rudimentary state of matter before the quintuplication process of the five elements takes place.

Tantras — Literally, "that which saves," they are a collection of scriptures, which, along with the Upanisads, Bhagavad Gita, Brahma-sutras, and others, make up the Sanatana Dharma — the eternal religion of India.

Tantric — Having to do with the Tantras, and specifically the worship of deities such as Vishnu, Siva, and Divine Mother.

Taparloka — The realm of seers and luminaries, the sixth of seven inward-reaching levels of consciousness, corresponding with the sixth chakra, the Ajna.

Tapasya — Rigorous spiritual disciplines, called austerities; one of the five niyamas of Yoga.

Tat — "That," in reference to Brahman or Reality.

Tathagatagarbha — That unlimited Consciousness that appeared in a human form, transcended it, and came again in a state of perpetual Freedom; a name for Lord Buddha.

Tattva — A wisdom principle, which, when meditated upon with the purified mind and intellect, releases profound insight contributing to the attainment of Samadhi.

Tattvas — Relating to the Twenty-four Cosmic Principles listed in the Sankhya Philosophy of Lord Kapila, which profoundly influenced all of India's major darshanas such as Buddhism, Yoga, and Vedanta.

Tejas — The light of refined Awareness; radiance.

Triputis — Triple principles that are fundamental in teaching spiritual truths.

Turiya — Literally, "The Fourth," referring to the fourth state of Awareness beyond waking, dreaming, and deep sleep. It is synonymous with the highest Samadhi, i.e., Asamprajnata in Yoga and Nirvikalpa in Vedanta.

Uddhava Gita — A profound scripture of India, which relates the teachings given by Sri Krishna to His beloved disciple, Uddhava.

Udghata — A force of spiritual awakening which is a precursor to the actual rising of Kundalini Shakti. It is an intrinsic testing mechanism which naturally measures whether the aspirant is ready and prepared for higher spiritual states, i.e., rising to the higher chakras.

Upadhis — Coverings or sheaths, signifying the five layers of gross and subtle matter hiding the abiding presence of Atman in living beings, i.e., body, life-force, mind, intellect, and ego.

Upanisad — The distillation of Vedic Wisdom, specifically around nondualism or Advaita. The word has been defined as "the proximity to the spiritual luminary which loosens the knot of ignorance and ushers in freedom."

Upanisads — A collection of 108 still-existing scriptures of Mother India, considered as primary scriptures, which must be heard.

Upekshanam — Equanimity of mind.

Utpatti — Origins, connected to the inner search for the causes of all effects in relativity.

Vaichitra — One of the Evolutes of Maya, it confuses and distracts the mind due to thinking about too many varieties of things.

Vairagyam — Detachment, or dispassion, which forms one of the four key practices of Vedanta. In it the sadhaka first masters discrimination between what is real and what is unreal, and then detaches from the latter.

Vak — Word, referring to those power-laden words which make up the scriptures and the guru's discourses containing wisdom transmission.

Vasishtha — The famous ancient rishi of India who was one of the mind-born sons of Lord Brahma, and who transmitted profound teachings to the Avatar, Sri Ram, when he was just a teenager.

Vedas — The four cardinal scriptures of the ancient Indians of the Vedic period, out of which the later Upanisads developed. The Upanisads form the fourth section of the Vedas, the first three consisting of rites and rituals, hymns and devotional songs, and rules for those who retire to the forest after earthly life is fulfilled to practice spiritual disciplines.

Vedanta — One of the Six Orthodox systems of philosophy in India, brought to the West by Swami Vivekananda in 1893. It is based upon the Vedas, but is a condensation of all that is found in them, as well as a maturation of the nondual essence of them.

Vedavyasa — Looked upon as "the Father of Vedanta," he collected many of the ancient scriptures of India upon the turning of an age, and thereby saved them from possible extinction.

Videhamukti — Liberation of the disembodied kind, wherein the soul enters into the formless state, seldom to return.

Vidyashastra — Knowledge of the revealed scriptures; one of the three sources and proofs of spiritual life and realization.

Vighna — Impediments along the spiritual path.

Vikalpa — Habitual desire-based mental projection.

Vindusthan — Another name for the Sahasrara Chakra.

Vishnu — The Lord of Sustenance who, along with Brahma and

Siva, form the divine Trinity of India.

Vishuddha Chakra — The fifth chakra, associated in physical terms with the region of the throat, but specifically aligned inwardly with the realm of Janaloka.

Vivarta — False superimposition of one thing over another, as in the covering of the Atman by the five sheaths, though Atman remains as changeless Reality.

Viveka — Discrimination, or discernment, which forms the first of four great practices in Vedanta (Sadhanachatushtaya) by which the aspirant learns to separate the essential from the nonessential. Its acquisition signals the beginning of true spiritual life and real attainment.

Vivekachudamani — The profound scripture by Shankara, perhaps his most well-known which transmits many of the foremost teachings of Vedanta in its 580 nectar-like slokas.

Vrittis — Mental vibrations, or waves; thought-forms.

Vyakti-upasanadhyana — Meditation on God with Form.

Vyavaharika — Relativity; what is empirical and ephemeral; worldly life devoid of spiritual teachings.

Yamas — Five preliminary practices in Yoga – nonviolence, truthfulness, nonstealing, continence, and nonreceiving of gifts – which form the basis for early spiritual discipline in traditional Yoga, i.e., ahimsa, satyam, asteya, brahmacharya, and aparigraha; also, the ten yamas of Tantric practice.

Yoga — The overall practice of spirituality, which is also the goal of embodied beings seeking to realize Truth and Self.

Yogas — Referring to the four main yogas, namely, Raja, Jnana, Bhakti, and Karma, but inclusive of a host of others — such as Kundalini Yoga.

Yogi — One who is practicing or has mastered the Eight-Limbed Yoga.

Yoginis — Women practitioners and adepts of the Yoga darshana.

Yuga — One of four ages or extended phases of time, which, when placed together end on end, make up what is termed a Mahayuga — individually called Satya Yuga, Treta Yuga, Dvapara Yuga, and Kali Yuga in order of manifestation.

SRV Associations of Oregon, San Francisco, and Hawaii

Other Books by Babaji Bob Kindler
- Twenty-Four Aspects of Mother Kali
    (Kindle edition e-book available)
- The Ten Divine Articles of Sri Durga
- The Avadhut and His Twenty-Four Teachers in Nature
- Sri Sarada Vijnanagita
- An Extensive Anthology of Sri Ramakrishna's Stories
- Swami Vivekananda Vijnanagita
- A Quintessential Yoga Vasishtha
- Reclaiming Kundalini Yoga

Mini Series
- We Are Atman All-Abiding:
- Strike Off Thy Fetters!
- Hasta-Amalaka Stotram

Planned Future Releases
- Footfalls of the Indian Rishis:
    Charting the Scriptures of Sacred Mother India
- The Nine Limbs of Bhakti of Sri Ram
- Visions of the Goddess:
    Commentaries on the Ecstatic Songs of Ramprasad
- Guru Yoga in Contemporary Times
- White Crane, White Swan

Further inquiries at:
SRV Associations
P.O. Box 1364
Honoka'a, Hawaii 96727

website: www.srv.org
email: srvinfo@srv.org

www.ingramcontent.com/pod-product-compliance
Lightning Source LLC
Chambersburg PA
CBHW070952080526
44587CB00015B/2277